Renewing the Mind

Renewing the Mind

Counselling and the Holy Spirit

Tony Dale

Marshall Pickering

Marshall Morgan and Scott
Marshall Pickering
3 Beggarwood Lane, Basingstoke, Hants RG23 7LP, UK

Copyright © 1987 by Tony Dale
First published in 1987 by Marshall Morgan and Scott
Publications Ltd
Part of the Marshall Pickering Holdings Group
A subsidiary of the Zondervan Corporation

British Library CIP Data

Dale, Tony
  Renewing the mind: counselling and the
  Holy Spirit.
  1. Pastoral counselling
  I. Title
  253.5   BV4012.2

  ISBN 0-551-01381-8

Text Set in Plantin by Brian Robinson, Buckingham.
Printed in Great Britain by Anchor Brendon Ltd, Tiptree,
Essex.

Contents

Introduction   7

 1: The Sick Need a Physician   11
 2: Who Sets the Standard?   16
 3: Relying on the Holy Spirit   25
 4: Where is the Battlefield?   39
 5: The Battlefield is the Mind   50
 6: Satan's Attack   62
 7: Our Weapons   72
 8: Depression   85
 9: Fears and Phobias   100
10: Sexuality   113
11: Epilepsy and Psychotic Illness   127
12: The Power of Signs and Wonders   145
13: The Needy you have Always   151

An Introduction to Caring Professions Concern   155

Introduction

I don't know how many times I have had people say to me when they find out that I am a doctor, 'Oh, Dr Dale, would you mind telling me what you think about . . .' It seems that the very word 'doctor' magically unlocks people's usual inhibitions about sharing their own deepest needs. Over the years, both in the surgery, and in church and conference work, I have found that the Holy Spirit has taught me much in the realm of helping people with their problems. Therefore, when pressed by the publishers of this book to try to set out some of these things in print, I felt that the Lord would have me give it a try.

A number of very helpful books have recently come out that deal with different aspects of counselling. When I first began to consider seriously writing this book, I almost gave up because I saw the quality of some of the other books on the market. Would this just be a case of 'be warned: the writing of many books is endless, and excessive devotion to books is wearying to the body' (Eccles. 12:12)?

I found the courage to proceed because none of the books that I came across seemed to deal with the areas I am attempting to deal with. In view of this, it is worthwhile to briefly define the scope of this book.

This is not a comprehensive textbook of Christian medical opinion on counselling. I am not a psychiatrist. I am really not a specialist at all. The fact that I am a doctor means that many people have come to me with problems, and I have been left trying to help them find answers. This book goes into what I have been learning by trial and error over the last few years.

It is important to say that this book will make little sense to those who do not see the importance of spiritual things in contributing to the way that all people tick. The baptism in the Holy Spirit was my introduction to Christian counselling. It seemed that following this experience, people kept coming to me and the Lord kept meeting with them. That is why you will find throughout the book a strong emphasis on the role of the Holy Spirit, and the necessity of the supernatural power of God breaking through into our counselling. People do not come to us just for good advice. They come because they believe that through us they can begin to find the answers to the deep questions and worries that perplex them. Those questions will only find their ultimate answer in God.

Not being a trained psychiatrist, I cannot claim to have given even a rudimentary introduction to the whole area of mental illness. Those who are looking for a medical textbook with a Christian emphasis will have to look elsewhere.

People come for counsel in virtually every area involved in complexities of modern living. I believe, as will come out clearly throughout this book, that the foundation for helping people find answers to their questionings is in the Bible. Whether the problem is in marriage, in the bringing up of children, in finances, in relationships, in the past, in the present, or even fears of the future, the answer lies in God and in His word.

Because I had neither the expertise nor the space available in a book of this size to tackle a wide variety of subjects, I have limited myself to those areas in which I have developed a special interest. The main thing that ties these areas together is that in each of them I happen to have seen quite a number of different people with similar problems.

All work that involves dealing with people and their problems is of necessity very personal. I have written to all those whose story might possibly be recognisable to obtain their permission to use it. All of the stories are true, but I have often changed names and places to protect the people concerned. I do thank them for their willingness to risk recognition by friends and family in the stories told. Their real life experiences will, I believe, teach all of us much.

My wife, Felicity, and I do much of our learning and counselling together, when time and family commitments allow it. She has been the leader in many of the areas that I have touched on in this book. It is such a joy to find the Lord teaching us together as a couple. In many senses she has co-authored this book, both by her many comments made in my writing of it, and by her direct experiences of helping many people.

All quotes from Scripture in this book are taken from the New American Standard Version of the Bible (NASV), which is published by the Lockman Foundation. Other versions are only used where specifically indicated.

My prayer in the writing of this book is that the following observations and stories from our experiences will help many to come to a greater dependence on the Lord Jesus Christ. We all have access to the same teacher, the Holy Spirit. We can all open the same textbook, the Bible.

1: The Sick Need a Physician

'And the news about Him went out into all Syria; and they brought to Him all who were ill, taken with various diseases and pains, demoniacs, epileptics, paralytics; and He healed them.' (Mt. 4:24).

Thursday mornings are much the same as any other morning in my surgery. On this particular morning, things had got off to a rather slow start. To be honest, I really wasn't concentrating that much because I knew that I was finishing at lunch time to help get things ready for our family holiday beginning the next day. First we were going to be heading up to North Wales for a conference, then we were going to be staying at a friend's cottage for most of the next three weeks.

My holiday reverie was interrupted by the surgery intercom on my desk. 'Dr Dale,' the receptionist said, 'There is a young doctor waiting here in reception who says that you arranged for him to spend the morning with you in surgery.'

'Help!' I thought to myself. I had completely forgotten that I had arranged for Sam to join my surgery for this morning. He was just coming up to the end of his GP training scheme, and wanted to see how a Christian doctor functioned in the surgery. It was time for some quick praying.

'Lord, you know that I want to be available to you this morning. Please bring in just the right patients for Sam and me to learn all that you want us to. I would love Sam to feel that his time with me has been worthwhile, Lord.'

A cup of coffee and two patients later, I had a growing feeling that the Lord had heard my prayer. He never wastes our time. This gave me the confidence to believe that the Lord was again going to use the surgery time for His glory. Often I had seen the Lord do this in the past. In fact it was now becoming my expected norm, rather than an unusual occurrence to see the Lord move clearly through the work that I was doing in the surgery.

The next patient in was completely new to me. She usually went to one of my partners, but as he was on holiday she had come into me this time. As she was only asking for a repeat prescription of the Pill I had no reason to think this would take long. On checking through her notes I saw that she was due for the annual check-up that we give all women on the Pill in our practice. While taking her blood pressure we began to chat. She was not married, but had been with her boyfriend for some considerable time. Her work was demanding. She was one of the managing directors in a large business further north. She did not feel at all ready to plan towards having a family. Anyway, her father had died suddenly two years previously and this had left her feeling quite insecure. In fact, since that time she had noticed that she was pretty fearful at times, and had herself become very anxious about death.

Sam and I looked at each other. I now knew why the Lord had allowed her to come to see me on this particular morning. The Holy Spirit flashed into my mind the verses in Hebrews, 'Since then the children share in flesh and blood; He Himself likewise also partook of the same, that through death He might render powerless him who had the power of death, that is, the devil, and might deliver those who through fear of death were subject to slavery all their lives' (Heb. 2:14-15).

As I began to talk to her along these lines we were soon deep into a discussion on spiritual things, and her own spiritual needs. She knew that there was much more to life than what she was experiencing at the moment, and was very hungry to learn more of how Jesus could step in and bring clear meaning and direction to her life.

She ended the conversation with a warm smile, thanking me for my concern, and saying that she would think very seriously about coming to church with me at some point in the near future.

An older man with chronic bronchitis, followed by a couple of women with their children took up the next fifteen minutes. Then Mark walked in.

Mark was well known to me because I had been seeing him frequently over the previous couple of months. He came originally from Tanzania, but in his student days had spent some time in Kenya. He had been quite actively involved in politics while there, and as such had made himself *persona non grata* to the authorities at home. His family had received a variety of threats. One of his brothers actually had to leave the country for his own safety.

Mark had been coming to see me because of a worrying pain in his chest. We had investigated him extensively (as had a previous GP who had been looking after him before he moved south to London) and found nothing physically wrong. The local chest hospital had also seen him, and shared our impression that the problem was not physical, but psychological. Mark was under threat of a deportation order from the Home Secretary, as his temporary visa had run out. He was genuinely scared that he might be forced to go back to Tanzania, and had no idea what would be his fate if he were to return.

On a previous visit to the surgery I had found out that he was reading Norman Vincent Peale's *The Power of Positive Thinking*. We had talked about this book quite a lot as I had also read it many years previously. In our chatting together, it had transpired that Mark was doing a lot of thinking about spiritual things.

Today the same story was coming out. Crushing central chest pain. A sense of anxiety for much of the time. The fear was present because a brother had died from cardiac problems two years previously. Mark wanted to know if I would think about sending him to another specialist who might be able to get to the bottom of his symptoms.

I knew that to do as he was asking would be both to waste his time and the time of the new specialist. Again I began to counsel him that the answers that he needed to find were going to have to come from a stronger source than medicine. We talked of how Jesus 'went about doing good, and healing all who were oppressed by the devil, for God was with Him' (Acts 10:38).

I suggested that Sam (who had been in the surgery with me throughout these conversations) and I should pray for him. Mark was most appreciative of that idea. As I began to pray and to lay hands on him he began to cry. We continued to pray. After a while the crying subsided and Mark left the surgery, thanking us profusely. Together Sam and I thanked the Lord for bringing this needy young man to us on this particular day. Had he come the next day, I would have missed meeting him.

Several more interesting people came through the surgery over the next half an hour. With most it was just a question of needing a medical certificate. We found others who just wanted someone to talk to about their personal needs. One man came in looking quite seriously ill, and after a thorough examination had to be transferred for an urgent appointment at the local hospital, as his symptoms led me to believe that he probably had cancer.

The surgery drew to a close and the receptionist brought in coffee. Sam and I began to chat about what we had seen that morning. Apart from the seriousness of some of the illnesses, we both commented on the other 'pains' that people had come with. It was plain to see why Jesus Himself said, 'It is the sick who need a physician'.

Here they were coming in with pains in the chest, pains in the abdomen, pains in the mind, and pains in the heart (which were not always physical pains); all needing to find peace and security. This, for many, will never be found in pills and potions, but only in a deep encounter with the Living God.

2: Who Sets the Standard?

'All Scripture is inspired by God and profitable for teaching, for reproof, for correction, for training in righteousness' (2 Tim. 3:16).

Over the years, the medical profession has put in so much work to try to understand what makes people tick. Yet it has paid little if any attention to the one book that could unlock what people are all about. Doctors spend years learning about intricate biochemical cycles, and complex nerve pathways, but no-one teaches them from the one true source of knowledge, the Bible. The Bible says that the 'fear of the Lord is the beginning of wisdom, and knowledge of the Holy One is understanding' (Prov. 9:10).

Over the last few years, there has been an increasing recognition within medical circles of the importance of the relationship between the mind and the body. However, even this encouraging integration of two parts of our make-up is still deficient. The Bible says that we are composed of spirit, soul and body. To leave out the spirit is to leave out the core of our being. If we do not have a clear understanding of the relationship of the realm of the spirit to the realm of the soul and body, then we will hardly begin to understand the nature of sickness, sin, or evil of any sort.

In any field of study, the so-called foundation subjects are absolutely vital. But can we have a foundation that leaves out the Word of God? Paul said in his first letter to the Corinthian church, 'For no man can lay a foundation other than the one which is laid, which is in Christ Jesus' (1 Cor. 3-11). Where we start from makes all the difference to where we end up. It is not enough to have some rough idea of where you want to go. We also need to have a clear idea of where we began.

Many philosophers have looked into these questions, but the answers were already given by a man who lived and who still lives. Jesus said, 'I know where I have come from and where I am going' (Jn. 8:14). His frequent references to His life with His Father, to his impending death, and then His glorious resurrection, all confirmed the reality of what He claimed.

It is our answers to these questions, the possibly unthought presuppositions behind our study of any subject, that in time determines how we will try to deal with people. If people have just 'happened', then in a sense it does not matter too much what 'happens' next. But if we are all here with a purpose, and behind that purpose there is a God who loves us, then it is vital that we deal with people with the loving consideration they need and deserve.

But who is to determine what foundations we start from?

Since the garden of Eden, we have had available to us the possibility of learning without having to make direct reference to God. We can learn from the Tree of Life or from the tree of the knowledge of good and evil. Mere facts are not enough. If knowledge is considered as the acquisition of information, then wisdom is the ability to apply that information properly.

Because of our intrinsic nature, if we are given the option of living without God then many of us will do just that. Who wants to have someone else interfering in what they do if they can, in the words of the famous pop song, 'do it

17

my way'? However, doing things our way, rather than God's way can only lead to the same result as was promised to Adam and Eve: 'In the day that you eat of it (the tree of the knowledge of good and evil) you shall surely die' (Gen. 2:17).

Because this death did not lead to immediate physical death, many have discounted the whole story. But that is to misunderstand what the Lord was doing here. Sin had entered and with it the whole potential of death. From that time onwards people were dying. The contrast with what the Lord had intended for mankind is exemplified in Jesus' words, 'I am come that you might have life and that you might have it more abundantly' (Jn. 10:10).

To think that we can understand human nature, without understanding the God who made men and women is both arrogant and foolish. People would like to think that you can arrive at 'truth' without needing to make any moral judgements, but this is not the case. All of our 'scientific' study has moral consequences. The apostle Paul makes this very clear in Romans 1:18, 'For the wrath of God is revealed from heaven against all ungodliness and unrighteousness of men, who suppress the truth in unrighteousness.'

When we try to understand people outside the context of the real and active involvement of God then we are leaving out a vital dimension of their being. Each part of a person is going to have a profound impact on the other parts of that person's make-up. We cannot touch the body without touching the emotions, any more than we can touch the spiritual part of a person and expect it to have no consequences on the realm of the soul and body.

In the way medicine is taught today, it is as if everyone has gone to look for answers anywhere and everywhere except for the one place where they can be found. 'In Him

18

are hid all the treasures of wisdom and knowledge' (Col. 2:3). It is small wonder that many hardly know where to start in trying to help people. They have refused to start at the one place where all knowledge and wisdom start. If it is true - as it certainly is - that 'the fool has said in his heart, "There is no God" ', then it is equally true that 'The fear of the Lord is the beginning of wisdom, and the knowledge of the Holy One is understanding' (Prov. 9:10).

An example that a GP friend of mine told me recently from his experience will help to underline these points. He had gone to a postgraduate seminar for local GPs in the nearby university medical school. On that day the subject was dermatology, and more specifically, eczema. The consultant doing the ward round took them to see some patients with intractable eczema. She described the various standard treatments, and her own success or lack of it at times in dealing with this condition. My friend asked if she ever used less specifically 'medical' approaches to try to help patients. He was astounded by her reply.

The previous week she had discharged a woman patient in her mid-forties with the following story. This woman had begun having problems with eczema in her early twenties. Over the years the eczema had become increasingly severe and more recently had led to her hospitalisation under another local consultant. This consultant, feeling that he had not really been able to help her had asked the lecturer if she would try to help. The patient had been brought onto her ward, where the doctor took time to go back to the roots of her patient's situation. Apparently, she had given birth to a handicapped child, when in her early twenties. Feeling that she could not cope with the pressures that this brought into her home, she arranged for the child to be put into care. This, however, led to strong feelings of guilt and failure, with which she had never been able to come to terms. Some time later her eczema had begun. She had never associated the two.

The consultant began to tell her about the love of God, and how we can come to true repentance and receive forgiveness for the sins and mistaken decisions of our past. The patient responded very warmly to this, and gave her life to the Lord. Within two days, the eczema had gone and she was discharged from the hospital.

Hebrews 4:12 states, 'For the word of God is living and active and sharper than any two-edged sword, and piercing as far as the division of soul and spirit, of both joints and marrow, and able to judge (discern) the thoughts and intentions of the heart. And there is no creature hidden from His sight, but all things are open and laid bare to the eyes of Him with whom we have to do.' Nothing remains hidden from the Holy Spirit. These concepts are put another way in 1 Corinthians 2:10-11, 'For the Spirit searches all things, even the depths of God. For who among men knows the thoughts of a man except the spirit of the man, which is in him? Even so, the thoughts of God no-one knows except the Spirit of God.'

The word of God is able to discern the thoughts and intentions of the heart. The Spirit of God is able to search our hearts. And we can, as we allow ourselves to be matured through the word and through the Spirit, learn how by 'practice (to) have (our) senses trained to discern good and evil' (Heb. 5:14).

Many Christians are not prepared for the discipline and hard work that are necessary in order to come into a deeper understanding of the word of God. There are no short cuts. I know when I was studying my medical textbooks that at times it seemed as if I would never get to the end of them. Late nights and early mornings often had to be the rule so that the work could be done. Can we apply a lesser standard to our coming to know and understand the book of life? It is as if we want to receive everything on the cheap nowadays. Our generation, that has grown up on instant coffee, tea bags, and TV dinners, expects to receive from the word of the Lord in the same way. It comes as a rebuke when we come across such verses as Jeremiah 7:13, 'and I spoke to you, rising up early and speaking, but you did not hear, and I called you but you did not answer'.

The Bible is *the textbook*. 'In Him was life, and the life was the light of men. And the light shines in the darkness, and the darkness did not overpower it' (Jn. 1:4-5). Jesus is the living embodiment of the written word of God. No wonder when people came to Him for counsel they so often found themselves astounded by what He said to them. 'For He was teaching them as one having authority, and not as the scribes' (Mk. 1:22).

If we want to understand about electricity, we will probably go to some basic textbook of physics. Likewise, when we want to understand people, we must go to the Book that describes them, the Bible. In it we will find the truth about human beings and the truth about God.

The Bible is not like other textbooks. It can only be truly understood when those reading it are themselves enlightened by the same Holy Spirit who inspired it. Reading it without the presence of the Holy Spirit leads to frustration and dryness – 'for the letter kills'. However, when prayerfully reading with the guiding of the Holy Spirit to open our spiritual eyes we find that the Bible it is a 'lamp to our feet and a light to our path' (2 Cor. 3:6; Ps. 119:105).

When we need answers, then we need to go to someone with the authority to give them to us. That someone is the Lord Jesus Christ. The basic way that we know His will is through the truths that are clearly shown in His word.

There are two main schools of thought when it comes to

counselling, that is, helping people through the various problems that they face. The predominantly held view in most secular and many religious circles is what is described as 'Nondirective Counselling'. Here no specific attempt is made to provide the answers. Rather, those needing help are encouraged to bring out the problems, look at the alternatives, and then to decide for themselves what is going to be the best way through this particular problem.

While this approach may be of some help in enabling people to admit that they have a problem, it is unlikely to bring much help in finding the answers. Often people will know that they have a deep need or hurt, but they do not know how to deal with it. They are looking for some clear guidance.

Jesus did not seem to have any qualms about telling people that they must change. However, He was always present with them to show them that the power to change was available, not from within themselves, but from the limitless power of God. Jesus always moved in the power of the Holy Spirit. He also made sure that those coming to Him knew that they too could draw on this same power.

This would be the truest expression of what most would nowadays call 'Directive Counselling'. The direction here, however, is not just the wisdom that the counsellor may be able to put into the counselling situation, but the word of the Lord for the person as stated by the Holy Spirit for that situation.

It often amazes me to have Christians coming to me for counsel in situations where the word of God is already so clear. An example of this would be the Christian young person who has fallen in love with someone who is not a Christian.

'Do you think that it would be right for me to marry her? I know that she is really close to giving her life to the Lord.'

But what do we do about the clear word of counsel in the Scriptures: 'Do not be bound together with unbelievers, for what partnership have righteousness and lawlessness, or what fellowship has light with darkness?' (2 Cor. 6:14).

It is not enough to say, 'the Lord has shown me that I am to marry so and so'. We must also see that we are moving within the confines that have been laid down for the Christian in the Bible. Our subjective feelings must be tempered by the objective truth as stated in God's word.

It was the Pentecostal leader Donald Gee, I believe, who gave us the following helpful quotation:

'All word - No Spirit - We dry up.
All Spirit - No word - We blow up.
Both Spirit and Word - And we grow up.'

To counsel from the authority of Scripture will bring the truth into people's lives, but may easily make them feel condemned, and leave them powerless to know what they can do to change. To counsel from the Bible in the power of the Holy Spirit will not only show the way, but also provide the power to effect the changes.

A young girl came to see me who was finding it very difficult to grow in her Christian life. She had been given many opportunities to learn from the Lord and had at one stage been involved in an excellent church. However, she had a boyfriend who was not a Christian. Each step forward in her walk with the Lord seemed to be matched by at least one step backwards.

I talked to her about the Lord's teaching on relationships and standards. This had the effect of rather frightening her, and so she again left her church. But the Holy Spirit had certainly not stopped speaking to her. When she reappeared some time later, she had not only broken off the harmful relationship, but had also let go of some other areas that were holding her back from the Lord. Her growth in the Lord now is something beautiful to watch.

Jesus made it plain that He had come to give us true life. To talk about counsel without an express desire to lead people into a closer relationship with the living God seems to me to be a contradiction in terms. 'In him was life and the life was the light of men.' (Jn. 1:4) refers to every part of our lives. When Jesus counselled He was invariably giving a portion of Himself, sharing His own life with those in need.

This ministry that Jesus so clearly fulfilled through His own life is now to be fulfilled through His body, the Church. We can do the task only if we are clearly led by the Holy Spirit. Our reference book is the Bible.

3: Relying on the Holy Spirit

'Then Jesus was led up by the Spirit' (Mt. 4:1).

Many will have heard the following story that was recently told by John Wimber of the Vineyard Fellowship in California. He was travelling by jet to speak at a Christian conference. While on the flight, he noticed the person across the aisle from him. The Lord put into John's mind, just like clear writing across a television screen, the word 'adultery' and then the name of a woman. John realised that the Lord was showing him the need for repentance in this man, and so leaned across the aisle and whispered to the man, 'I need to talk to you about ....' naming the woman that the Lord had put into his mind. The man was dumbstruck! Needless to say he was quite prepared to talk to John. Their talk resulted in the man coming to repentance and giving his life to the Lord Jesus.

This is a dramatic example of what many Christians are coming to see as an indispensable part of their Christian armoury: namely, moving in the gifts of the Holy Spirit.

Jesus seemed to be as much at ease talking with the parents of an epileptic boy, as with a grieving mother over her lost son, or with a woman caught in the very act of adultery. How did He know how to respond to these people in need? Why was his advice always spot on?

His secret was that he was always being perfectly led by

the Spirit of God. And this same gift is available to us. Paul tells us in Romans 8 that it is 'all who are being led by the Spirit of God, these are sons of God'.

A young woman came into my surgery to ask me for a repeat prescription of the Pill. I had not met her before and so was chatting with her to put her at her ease. It quickly turned out that she was the wife of a Christian worker who had just moved into the area where I was then working.

As she got up to leave, I noticed that she looked slightly strained.

'Is everything OK?' I asked, 'You seem to have a weight on your mind.' Suddenly she appeared to brighten up. 'Oh no, I'm fine thank you.'

Before I could even think what I was saying I heard myself say to her, 'You have just had an abortion, haven't you? That is why you feel like you have the world on your shoulders.'

She sat down and burst into tears. She wanted to know how I had known as she hadn't told anyone, and she and her husband had only just moved into the area. I didn't really know myself how I had known. I did not have any old notes as she had not been on my list for long enough for her notes to have come through to me. As we began to talk, out came the story. A few months previously, before she and her husband were married, they had slept together and she had become pregnant. As they could not face the shame of this, and were shortly due to take on their new pastoral role, they decided she would have an abortion. Now the Lord had supernaturally brought this to the surface through one of the gifts of the Holy Spirit.

A short while ago I had another rather strange experience for a doctor in his surgery. A young woman came in and began telling me about the breakdown of her marriage relationship. It transpired that her husband had been battering her quite badly. As she poured out her tale I found my heart moved with compassion for her. Soon the tears began to flow. What on earth was happening to me? No self-respecting doctor would behave in this fashion.

As I struggled with my own emotions - the feeling of empathy with this patient - my mind went back to the words that had been spoken of the Lord Jesus: 'And seeing the multitudes, He felt compassion for them, because they were distressed and downcast like sheep without a shepherd' (Mt. 9:36). I knew that the Lord was letting me share in His own grief over what this woman was experiencing. How could I bring her the life of Jesus if I did not share any of His compassion for her needs?

This sort of experience obviously raises many questions regarding traditional views on 'professionalism'. We are taught that we should not be at all emotionally involved with those whom we are trying to help. Won't we find ourselves impossibly weighed down with everyone else's worries if we allow ourselves to identify in this fashion?

As I have tried to answer these questions to my own satisfaction, I have found it very hard to picture Jesus working as we would expect his modern day 'professional' counterpart to work. Surely He is our pattern in this, as He is in everything else. It was His very compassion which over and over again is recorded by the disciples in the gospels as the thing that they noticed most. Surely He was not treating people as the next 'case' to see before He would be free to move on to something or somebody else?

When the Lord gives us help He is giving us of Himself. 'For God so loved the world, that He gave us His only begotten Son. . .' We should only help people if we can act in a similar way. Jesus told us, 'As the Father has sent me, so send I you' (Jn. 20:21). It is not enough for us to offer people good advice. They can get that from books! It is not

27

even enough for us to offer them the truth from God's word, because devoid of the Spirit that very word can finish them off (2 Cor. 6:3). We need to bring them truth in the power of the Spirit. As God's word comes through us, people will sense the love of God moving through us to them.

How vital it is that we, like Jesus, have a clear idea of what the Father is wanting to do or say in any given situation! This would be impossible if we did not have the clear leading of the Holy Spirit.

Many Christians find it very difficult to distinguish between the leading of the Holy Spirit, and their own thoughts and ideas. I was greatly helped in this area by something I read in a book about David du Plessis. David was beginning to be led into the work which was to make him world famous as one of the forerunners of the Charismatic Movement. He was spending some time in praying in tongues, when he noticed that something was happening. As he spoke to God in tongues, he found that God was speaking back into him. As he continued to pray in this way he discovered that he was learning to differentiate between what were just his own thoughts and what was truly of the Holy Spirit.

About the same time I came across some very similar concepts in Oral Roberts's book, *A Daily Guide to Miracles*. This book contains a most helpful chapter on the use of the gift of tongues, which is described as 'We speak to God - He speaks to us'.

Often, as I am listening to people, I will be praying away in tongues under my breath. I am asking God to give me the wisdom to know how to help this person. Every person is different. We cannot rely on how we handled this situation last time we encountered it. The root need may be completely different. We, like Jesus, must only do 'what we see the Father doing' (Jn. 5:19).

At a recent meeting, my wife was helping a young woman who had come forward for prayer. The Holy Spirit clearly told her to ask the girl a series of questions. 'Were you frightened of your father at home? Did he physically abuse you? Was incest a problem within the family?' Although it was hard for the girl to face up to such questions they immediately stripped off the mask which she had been hiding behind. The Holy Spirit was able to show my wife how to lead this girl gently into a real place of forgiveness and healing.

Being led by the Holy Spirit is the privilege of all Christians. It does not need to be the province of a chosen few. Jesus told us that, 'when He, the Spirit of truth, comes, He will guide you into all the truth; for He will not speak on His own initiative, but whatever He hears, He will speak; and He will disclose to you what is to come' (Jn. 16-13).

Jesus is described by the prophet Isaiah as the 'Wonderful Counsellor'. This work of Jesus is now to be carried on by all who follow him through 'the Paraclete', the one called to help. This helper is the Holy Spirit.

The gifts of the Holy Spirit are like equipment that is needed by a soldier if he is to be able to fight effectively. We could use just our hands, but we are likely to find it difficult if we come across someone else with sword and shield! In the same way, we could use only natural reasoning and experience, but this may easily prove inadequate when we come face to face with our enemy, the devil. It is he who binds people's lives, and seeks to destroy their minds and emotions. We will find that we need the power of the Holy Spirit to win in this type of battle.

Another experience may help to draw some of these ideas together. I well remember a young woman who came into the ward that I was working on for an abortion. Although I did not approve of what was being done, I had little option but to see her onto the ward, and try to help her as best as I could. I was allowed to opt out of involvement in the actual operation.

When I went up to see her during my evening ward round, I found her eager to talk. Already she was having serious doubts about what she had done. It was obviously too late to reverse that, but I knew that I could talk to her about the Lord Jesus and His power to forgive. She was eager to learn, and soon we were at the point where she wanted to pray to ask the Lord Jesus to come into her life.

We tried to pray together, but I could not get her to pray. She would answer me when I spoke to her, but she could not seem to pray. She could not even pray by copying the words that I was using. This all seemed very strange to me, and I began to hear a few warning bells. At this point I felt the Holy Spirit prompt me to ask her if she had been involved in using ouija boards in the past. When she answered that she had had some casual contact I explained to her how this could affect her deeply at a spiritual level. She was keen for us to pray for her to be free. First we looked a little at what the Bible teaches in these areas. As I was pretty inexperienced at this sort of thing, especially on the ward, I felt rather apprehensive. But as soon as I began to pray and cut her free from these past experiences, she also began to pray. How thrilled she was to come into the Kingdom and to know that her sins were forgiven!

Objective truth is to be found in Scripture. It provides the framework by which we can share our faith and, under the leading of the Holy Spirit, see people reflected. Subjective leading by the Spirit will help us to personalise what Scripture is saying. However, this leading must be in conformity to the written word of God and never contrary to it. This balance between the working of the Holy Spirit and the necessity of our knowing and applying the word of God is seen clearly when we look at the area of discernment.

Discernment may be an expression of our maturity and understanding of the word of God. Equally it may be a supernatural manifestation of the Holy Spirit. It may also fall anywhere along the line that would connect those two.

I will try to illustrate this by the slightly differing ways that my wife and I would work in many situations. She is more intuitive than I am, and more sensitive to the prompting and leading of the Holy Spirit. I am probably more rational, relying more on what I know of the Scriptures and of the patterns that I have seen the Holy Spirit use in helping people. A person might come to see us, worried because of a variety of fears. Felicity may rapidly sense that there is an element of demonic oppression. She may sense the Holy Spirit saying to her that she needs to ask about any deliberate contact that the person has had with the occult.

I, though, may find myself thinking of the verse, 'For God has not given to us a spirit of fear' (2 Tim. 1:7). Knowing from past experience that fear is virtually always an area of enemy attack, I would want to know what had opened this person up to attack in this way. Two thoughts would quite naturally come to mind (or, you might say, were prompted by the Holy Spirit). 'Has this person had some occult contact, or have they been in a frightening situation that the devil has taken advantage of?'

Both approaches would lead one rapidly to the same conclusion. Both ways still leave one needing to act in the power of the Holy Spirit to see the person set free. Both approaches are complementary to each other.

True counselling is going to demand of us a new dependence on the Holy Spirit and a fresh living understanding of the Bible. One of the precious truths that we see the Holy Spirit breaking open to His Church in this generation is the reality of the priesthood of all believers. It is thrilling in a meeting to see each one of God's children taking an active role. How beautiful it is, as a time of ministry opens up after preaching, to see many involved in praying for the people beside them!

Jesus was led by the Holy Spirit. He was the most perfect example of a counsellor. It was Jesus who told us that it would be better for us if He were to return to His Father, so that the Holy Spirit could come alongside us and teach us how to live as He lived. As new covenant Christians we have the tremendous privilege of knowing the Holy Spirit. As Christians living in this particular generation we have the privilege of seeing the Holy Spirit move on a world-wide scale possibly greater than anything that has ever occurred before.

The call of God to each of us is to grow into maturity. It is time that we stopped being little boys and girls, and grew into the 'sons' that our heavenly Father can truly be proud of. We are either an example of what God is accomplishing through His Church, or we are a drain on the army of God. We are either numbered among the givers or among the receivers. Jesus said, 'It is more blessed to give than to receive' (Acts 20:35).

The context of this lovely saying of Jesus, quoted by the apostle Paul to the Ephesian Church leaders, is to encourage them to continue giving of themselves freely. All leadership within the Church demands a willing laying down of our lives for the lives of others. Any counsellors who are moving in the Holy Spirit are going to be learning to lay down their own opinions, so that the will of the Lord can shine through ever more clearly.

On one occasion I remember well my own need of advice. I was near the beginning of my second year at medical school. Felicity and I had just started going out together. The Lord was beginning to do good things within our year at the school, and I had recently been baptised in the Holy Spirit. Then, out of the blue, the Lord spoke to me clearly. I was to leave medical school and medicine, and He would show me what He wanted of me.

Could this really be the Lord? How well I remember talking about this with Felicity and another friend, Richard Thomas, who were in the same year as me. As I began to grapple with this question, what a source of strength it was to me to have two such friends alongside!

Nine months later, when I did actually leave medical school, the pathway was prepared for me by another medical student, Nick Cuthbert. The Lord had spoken quite independently to him to tell him that he was also to leave medical school. Virtually no-one stood with him at the time. Nearly all counselled him to the effect that he was making a big mistake. But God was preparing Nick for the special task that He had for him. Now Nick is mightily used by the Lord in evangelistic missions and teaching, not only in this country, but also abroad.

Later, when I had finished two years at a small Bible School, the Lord was to lead me equally clearly back to medical school. This time it was quite against my better judgement, but I knew it was the Lord's way for me because of the wise counsel of others whom the Lord had put around me.

As we seek to help others, we desperately need to know that we ourselves are being led by the Holy Spirit. Jesus told us that 'the sheep follow him, because they know his voice' (Jn. 10:4). As we learn to recognise the voice of the good shepherd, we in turn become good shepherds. It is only as we help others to hear *Him*, that we are going to help them at all.

This does not always mean that people know that they have heard the voice of the Lord. It does not necessarily mean either that they will want to respond to our counsel. We are, after all, only talking about giving counsel - not commands! There is a place for commands. There is a place for learning obedience within the body of Christ. But Christian counsellors who begin to give commands will soon find that they are moving into arrogance and error. People have to be helped to hear the voice of *the* good shepherd. He is the Lord.

A few years ago, when I had been out of medicine for three or four years because of work in our local church, one of my fellow elders began suggesting to me that the Lord might want me to go back to doing some medical work. I'm not fully sure why, but it never really rang any bells with me at that time. I often seem to need a hammer on the head before I notice the Lord is speaking to me!

A few months later, I was beginning to wonder myself if the Lord was wanting me to get back into some part-time medical work. I was a little apprehensive as I had been out of medicine for some time. Maybe that is why I hadn't listened before. Then out of the blue I was offered a partnership with a local group of doctors with whom I had had no previous contact. Should I take it? I was in quite a dilemma, and had to have clear answers within two weeks. I could not hear the Lord clearly for myself. So I went to another friend. He was quite specific with me. The Lord had spoken to him and I was to take it.

With considerable fear and trepidation I followed the advice. And it has all been so clearly the Lord's will. What a tragedy if, at this moment of my own need, I had been given not the word of the Lord, but human wisdom! We must be those who hear God, however He chooses to speak to us. When we hear we must obey. It is unlikely that the Lord is going to bother to keep speaking to us if we ignore what He has already said. Our obedience at each step is our preparation for the steps that are to follow. As we begin to rely on the Lord in our counselling, so He will show Himself more and more clearly to us.

The Bible tells us that as 'many as are led by the spirit of God are the sons of God' (Rom. 8:14). Do we know this leading? Without it we are really spending much of our time groping about in the dark. We need to be clear here. We believe in a supernatural God who is not only able to, but wants to speak to us. In reality, any speaking to us by God is supernatural. The realm of the spirit impinging on the realm of the natural is a supernatural manifestation of God.

When my wife and I have an important decision to make, we have found that the Lord has led us to adopt four simple steps to confirm that we are understanding Him correctly.

First, we expect the peace of God to guard our hearts (Phil. 4:6-7). This awareness of the peace of God deep within is really the fundamental level of our awareness of the Lord. It is the place of knowing the presence of God; the place where we are in communion with God. This peace can guard one's heart through the most difficult of circumstances. It is the peace that comes with the certainty that God has spoken.

However, our subjective experience of peace has not, for us, been enough to act on in major decisions in our lives. It is the foundation that we stand on when the decision has been made. It is our security if things seem subsequently to go wrong. But on its own, it is only the start to our knowing that we are acting in response to the promptings of God.

Secondly, we ask the Lord to speak to us clearly out of Scripture. Usually we would take a day or so to have time in fasting and prayer before the Lord. We would expect Him to speak to us individually through our study of the written word, or by putting into our hearts what passage we were to receive counsel from. We have begun to see that this leading from His word does not need to be vague. He is able to be remarkably specific with us if we let Him.

Thirdly, we ask the Lord for a supernatural sign. Our God dwells in the realm of the spirit. Surely he can allow this realm to break through to us so that we know our way forward? At times we have seen the Lord do remarkable things in this area to help us on the path towards making difficult decisions.

A few years ago we were in a situation where a Christian group that we were involved in owed a large sum of money, and had little prospect of being able to pay it back in either the short or long-term future. Felicity and I wondered if the Lord wanted us to sell something that was very precious to us (and quite valuable!), to help pay off the money owing. We were sitting in the regular Sunday morning meeting, when one of the young men stood up to share some of the things that the Lord had been teaching him on faith. At one point he was trying to illustrate how the Lord calls us to move out in faith.

'It would be rather like the Lord asking Tony and Flick to sell their (and here he named the valuable thing we had in mind) and to trust the Lord for future provision.'

We both looked at each other quite startled. He had no idea of what we had been praying and thinking about. Then as if the Lord wanted to underscore the point, he used exactly the same illustration again. We knew that the Lord was speaking to us personally!

On a more recent occasion the Lord was directing us in a major move of location and ministry. We knew that we could not make any moves until we were quite clear that this was really the Lord leading us. We decided to go over to see a friend whom we greatly respected and to discuss our plans with him. I did not know this at the time, but Felicity was praying in the car as we drove over. As she prayed, she asked the Lord if He would give us a supernatural sign by having our friend reply, when he heard of our plans, 'Oh, I've known for two years that the Lord was going to move you to that place.'

Sure enough, when we began to broach the subject with him his response was to reply in the exact words that Felicity had asked the Lord to give to him. I don't know who was more shocked, Felicity when she heard our friend's reply, or me when she explained to me that the Lord had answered her prayer for a supernatural sign.

Lastly, we always seek the confirmatory counsel of friends. The Book of Proverbs makes it clear that 'in an abundance of counsellors there is safety' (Prov. 11:14). We need friends who will be honest with us. We also need to value their advice, otherwise we may find it difficult to hear the Lord speaking to us through them. This does not mean that the advice one is given is always correct, but one would be quite wrong not to listen very carefully to what others, who are close to you and to the Lord, are saying.

I would not want to give the impression that I think everyone should be patterning their guidance from the Lord in the way that we have been led. Rather, I am aware from some of our mistakes, that there is great value in not being dependent alone on our own sense of what the Lord has spoken to us. It seems to me to be clear from Scripture that we should be maturing to a position where we have a clear confidence that we have actually known the Lord's voice. This may be by His inner witness within us, by vision or dream, through prophecy, or in any of the wide variety of ways that the Lord may choose to speak to us.

This, however, needs to be held in tension with the equally clear teaching of Scripture as to our own natural propensity to be deceived, especially if it is to our advantage! The counsel of others is a tremendous safeguard to hasty decision making. It is going to take time to find the others, confide in them, and for them to pray over the things that you are speaking about to them.

We probably don't understand ourselves very well if we don't realise that our hearts can still deceive us. Motivation is not always easy to sort out. Many times people will come to you wanting advice on things that they have already decided on in their own minds. It may be that the Lord wants you to raise questions of motivation into these situations. It is far better for us to judge ourselves firmly now, than subsequently to have to face the Lord's dealing with us over our faulty motives.

'Faithful are the wounds of a friend' (Prov. 27:6). How often when we or others risk a little wounding, we actually save ourselves from major injury! We can rely on the Holy Spirit to lead us clearly if we are willing to apply His clear guidelines in Scripture to the steps that we propose to take.

As we begin to understand the ways that the Holy Spirit leads us and teaches us through His word, so we are going to learn how we can be of most help to other people. Our growing awareness of the realm of the spirit teaches us also to be careful of the realm of demonic powers. It is into this area that we must look in the next chapter.

4: Where is the Battlefield?

'And be not conformed to this world, but be transformed by the renewing of your mind, that you may prove what the will of God is, that which is good and acceptable and perfect' (Rom. 12:2).

Sue first became known to me when she was transferred from the teaching hospital where she was in training, to our smaller, peripheral hospital. She had been in and out of the nurses' sick bay for some time. The doctor in charge of her case was becoming concerned that she might have to stop nursing.

Sue was experiencing strange blackouts, associated with severe abdominal pain. When she began her training these attacks had been very infrequent. Now they seemed to be happening more and more often. The physicians had extensively investigated her and drawn a complete blank. As usually happens in this situation the next stop was the psychiatrist. He gave her a clean bill of health also. But the blackouts and abdominal pains continued.

It was at this juncture that my consultant became involved. I was just the house officer on the ward and very junior. I had little idea what was happening to Sue. We again put her through a battery of tests, but had no more success than the teaching hospital that she had come from.

My consultant was a Christian and, as such, very concerned for Sue who was also a Christian. As, by this time, we had all developed quite a relationship with her, the consultant suggested that I might be willing to take her home to be with my wife and me for a few days. I think he hoped that in the home environment we might find something that could account for what was going on with Sue.

Felicity and I agreed to give it a try. Sue had been with us for a few days when Felicity asked the Lord what on earth was happening. Although Felicity is also a doctor, she then, as now, finds it easier to think outside the straight medical framework, and so to 'hear' what the Holy Spirit is saying to her

'Ask her if she hears voices,' the Holy Spirit told her. Rather surprised by this suggestion, but open to learn, Felicity did just this. Imagine her surprise when Sue replied that she did hear voices, but they had told her never to let anyone know about them!

We had had enough experience to know that this might be a demonic manifestation. So Felicity decided not to take it any further, but to wait until I came home.

With the evening free, we began to chat with Sue again. This time, having had the source of the problem opened up by the Holy Spirit, we could begin to probe into what was really happening. The following story emerged.

When she was fourteen, Sue had begun having these 'voices' talk to her. They were always very negative. She did not know what had started the voices. They had begun quite suddenly in the middle of a class at school. As time went on the voices became more and more insistent. They began to threaten her. They were constantly telling her that she should commit suicide. Sue discovered that she could get rid of the voices by blacking herself out. These blackouts were quite genuine, not faked. She began to find herself developing severe abdominal pain, on purpose as it were, and this would be followed by the blackout. When she came round, the voices would be gone - but only temporarily. All too quickly they were back, with their same persistant demands.

We did not know much about this sort of thing, but we had heard enough to know that this was certainly not from God. It is probably a good thing that at that point I knew little about classic psychiatric practice or I might easily have been diverted into classing this as a manifestation of schizophrenia and have decided to treat her accordingly. Jesus talked about how Satan has come to 'steal and kill and destroy' (Jn. 10:10), but He Himself has come that we 'might have life and might have it abundantly'. Sue needed this abundant life.

We offered to pray. A simple word of command in the name of Jesus and she was set free. On a couple of occasions over the next few days she felt the abdominal pain coming back. To begin with she was a little fearful that the voices would find a way to attack her again. But we taught her how to use the scriptures as a weapon against the enemy and how to use praise. She has never from that day to this (now about ten years) had a recurrence.

What can we understand from this story? The Bible describes us as triune beings, i.e. made up of three parts. 'Now may the God of peace Himself sanctify you entirely; and may your spirit and soul and body be preserved complete, without blame, at the coming of our Lord Jesus Christ' (1 Thess. 5:17). The apostle Paul shows us here, most clearly, that God is interested in all three parts of our make-up. One part of our being is going to affect the other parts.

Our Bodies

Our bodies are important! If we neglect our bodies we will find that they will begin to let us down. Often I have found that a good game of squash will actually revitalise me to have the energy to continue in a busy schedule. Excellent books, such as Trevor Martin's *Good Health* look more fully at this area.

When our bodies break down because of disease, we naturally want to experience the healing that is available to us in Christ. When Christ died for us he procured a full salvation. Salvation and wholeness are virtually synonymous in the New Testament. That is why Paul is asking the Lord to preserve us complete. This area is beautifully explained by FF Bosworth in his classic book, *Christ the Healer*.

The word 'Soteria' which is the Greek word for salvation, implies deliverance, preservation, healing, soundness and in the New Testament is applied sometimes to the soul and other times to the body only. The Greek word 'Sozo' translated 'saved' also means 'healed', 'made whole', 'made sound'. In Rom. 10:9 it is translated 'saved' and in Acts 14:9 the same word is translated 'healed', referring to the healing of the man lame from birth. The Greek words for 'salvation' and 'saved' mean both spiritual and physical salvation or in other words spiritual and physical healing.

This is not to imply that we will not grow old, or that our bodies are not subject to decay in much the same way as the rest of creation. What we do know though is that the death of Jesus has made the perfect provision for our every need. We may at present only experience this provision in part. This does not stop us reaching out for all that the Lord has for us!

Our Spirits

'The spirit of man is the lamp of the Lord, searching all of the innermost parts of his being' (Prov. 20:27).

Most Christians are at best dimly aware of the existence of their spirit. Our human spirit is the place where the Spirit of God mingles with our spirit to make us spiritually alive. When we are born again, it is by the Spirit of God making our human spirit alive. Prior to this our spirits were dead (Eph. 2:1).

One of the principle functions of the gift of tongues is to help us be aware of the realm of the Spirit. A person who uses the gift of tongues does find, as Paul says, that 'the mind is unfruitful.' However we are aware of being built up inwardly. In another place Paul describes this as being 'strengthened with might by His Spirit in the inner man'.

Watchman Nee in his classic work, *The Spiritual Man*, goes to great lengths to help us understand how these different parts of the human make-up function. He defines from Scripture the human spirit as being made up of conscience, intuition and communion. It is here that we commune with and learn from God. It is from this source that the various gifts and manifestations of the Holy Spirit are released within us. It is here that the 'rivers of living water' that Jesus spoke of are going to find their release into our lives. Life from God, passing through our spirit, will then affect our souls and our bodies.

Our Souls

Our soul, along with our spirit, is the eternal part of us, our real self, which is being shaped by the presence of Christ within us. The soul, which Watchman Nee shows to be made up of our mind, emotions and will, is the bridge between the natural and the spiritual. Here in the realm of the soul the choices are made that shape what we are going to become. Here in our thinking we allow ourselves to be formed either into the image of Christ, or progressively deformed into a dark shadow of what the Lord intended for us. Here, in the soul, the enemy seems to bring his most subtle attacks to try to destroy us.

How true it is, as stated by Solomon, 'For as man thinks within himself, so he is' (Prov. 23:7)! Our thoughts have the most profound influence on what we are and what we become. Whoever can find a way to control our thoughts will in time be able to shape what we are. Thoughts work themselves out in the physical in what we usually call psychosomatic illness. Many stomach ulcers, cardiac problems, tension type headaches, etc. show the powerful way in which what is going on in our minds can affect our bodies.

Similarly the mind becomes a link to the realm of the spirit, either the human spirit, the Holy Spirit, or to the realm of Satan and his demonic spirits. The Bible tells us that when we are tempted it is our own lusts that tempt us (Jas. 1-14). As we allow ourselves to think about the things that tempt us we find that we are shaped by these thoughts and 'when lust has conceived, it gives birth to sin; and when sin is accomplished, it brings forth death' (Jas. 1-15).

Our minds do not have to be such a negative influence upon our spiritual lives though. The injunction of Paul in Philippians 4:8 is that 'whatever is true, whatever is honourable, whatever is right, whatever is pure, whatever is lovely, whatever is of good repute, if there is any excellence and if anything worthy of praise, let your mind dwell on these things.' Obedience to these Scriptures will lead us into an experience of the promise that 'the mind set on the Spirit is life and peace' (Rom. 8:6).

Some years ago I spent some time working in a hospital pharmacy. I did not do anything very grand there. My work was to wash the intravenous infusion bottles. This involved sticking these bottles onto a brush which was driven by a small electric motor. All day long I washed hundreds of these bottles, and then refilled them with infusion fluid. I knew that I had to do the job carefully because of how the fluid would be used, but the work did not involve much brain power!

This left my mind free to learn to think 'on the things above, not on the things that are on earth' (Col. 3:2). This has subsequently had a profound impact on the way that I think and act. During those hours I tried to learn what Brother Lawrence in the fourteenth century called 'Practising the Presence of God'. I spent much time praying in tongues. Slowly some of the lessons that the Holy Spirit wanted to teach me about the reality of living in God's presence began to sink in.

It is possible to live in praise. King David was not just being poetic when he said, 'I will bless the Lord at all times, His praise shall continually be in my mouth' (Ps. 34:1).

These concepts are fundamental when one is trying to help others. So many people have thoughts about themselves that are basically negative. When the devil finds a way to muscle in on these thoughts, they become truly destructive.

While it may be true that 'the idle mind is the devil's playground', it is certainly true that 'the mind set on the flesh is death' (Rom. 8:6). For example, how often have you heard a person say, 'Well, I know that today is going to be an awful day'? You can be pretty sure that the day will end up just as they expect! It seems as if our very thoughts become the seedbed for the creation of the things that we either want or fear.

I have often found when counselling people that they

have allowed their minds to be filled with rubbish. People who have many bad dreams, whether they are sexually arousing, or nightmares, may well be choosing to fill their minds with junk. Those who are finding it difficult to control lustful thoughts may be preparing the very soil of their mind by reading books and magazines or newspapers which are continually arousing them. People who are finding that fear is an integral part of their lives may be watching the late night horror films on the television.

It would be naïve to assume that there is always a straight cause and effect relationship as I have suggested above, but, to deny that this is often the case is flying in the face of common sense and many people's experience. We do become like the things that we think about. It has been said that, 'We become like what we worship; and we worship what we think about most!'

The way that the devil finds access through our thoughts is most interestingly explained by Paul in Ephesians 4: 'Be angry, and yet do not sin; do not let the sun go down on your anger, and do not give the devil an opportunity'.

It seems that when we are angry, we are bordering very close to sin, though we may not have sinned yet. However, if we go to bed that night without letting go of the anger it will inevitably begin to turn into resentment. At this point it has become sin. Satan will then take this 'opportunity' to try to draw us further into sin and more resentment, or even revenge.

One can see this principle extending into all areas of what I shall call 'thought sin'. Most men will have experienced something along the following lines. You are walking through Soho (or your own city's red light district) when you catch sight of a picture of a striptease artist. Immediately your thoughts are stirred. You can at that point reject the thought. You can think on it a little - and then reject it. Or you can dwell on it.

If you take the last course of action it is only a very little time before you find other thoughts beginning to flood in.

'Why not go inside and see if the show is on?'

'Nobody will know. Why not see if they have any pornographic videos inside?'

It seems that the devil has some access that enables him to insert tempting thoughts into our minds that will push us along the path to destruction. We allow the initial train of thoughts, but he is more than willing to jump in and push us beyond the place that we would have originally intended to go.

I once heard Dr Peter Quinton expounding this passage from Ephesians 4. He said that giving the devil 'an opportunity' could be translated as giving him 'a landing pad'. It is as if our sin provides a small foothold onto which Satan will apply his tenacious grip. Given half a chance he will push us from 'thought sin' into 'active sin'.

There is so much mystery still tied into this whole area of how Satan has access to our thoughts. The importance of this will be looked at much more fully in the next chapter when we examine the nature of the spiritual warfare that is going on around us all of the time.

At a strictly physical level it appears to make sense that some biochemical transaction is taking place in our brain (the physical side of the mind) whenever we think. Experimentation that has been done shows that certain chemicals which scientists call neurotransmitters, will produce differing moods when applied to the appropriate parts of the brain. This is the basis of the action of neuro-pharmacologically active drugs, i.e. drugs that will work on the brain or central nervous system. This is why drugs, like the antidepressants that are very widely used, seem to have a clear, beneficial effect in many cases. However, it is probably a mistake to assume, as some do, that this implies that the cause of the depression in first place was a physical lack of this particular chemical in the brain.

An interesting example of this tie-in between the physical, the realm of the mind and the realm of the spirit is seen in certain cases where people have epilepsy. Normally these people are well controlled on anti-epileptic drugs.

Deeper investigation of some of these folk, though, has shown a clear spiritual starting place for the epilepsy. Possibly this begins following some occult contact, or even through a fear of epilepsy. Sometimes, when seeing the spiritual basis of the epilepsy, we have been able to deal with the demonic presence that is causing the fits. This has rendered the sufferers free from subsequent fits, and able to come off their drugs.

Why a drug should apparently be able to control some manifestations of demonic activity I do not know. What I do know is that people can be instantly set free from demonic activity through the authority that we have in the name of Jesus.

It is worth our while summarising these ideas before going on to look more fully at the battle that goes on to control our minds. It is clear that Satan does have some access to our thinking. It is equally clear that our thinking is going to have a profound effect on what we are and on what we will become.

At the start of this chapter we saw that we are 'transformed by the renewing of (our) minds'. Most people who come to us for counsel are going to need some help to change the way that they think. They may view themselves as excessively fat, even when they are in fact dangerously thin - as in anorexia nervosa. They may have an external facade that gives the appearance of boundless self-confidence, even while inside they are not sure how they are going to hold things together enough to carry on with their work. They may be one of the leaders in the Church, apparently preaching and teaching under the anointing of the Holy Spirit, and yet grappling with the guilt brought on by an as yet unconfessed adulterous affair that they have not been able to deal with.

As God's truth grips their minds, they can be set free. As God's truth grips us, we can also be set free.

5: The Battlefield is the Mind

'For though we walk in the flesh, we do not war according to the flesh, for the weapons of our warfare are not of the flesh, but are divinely powerful for the destruction of fortresses. We are destroying speculations and every lofty thing raised up against the knowledge of God, and we are taking every thought captive to the obedience of Christ' (2 Cor. 10:3-5).

We need to understand what is going on in the mind in spiritual warfare. It is here that most people needing counsel are found to be so vulnerable. The above text gives us our starting place.

The three areas that need to be destroyed are all in the mind. These are the areas of 1) speculations; 2) every lofty thing raised up against the knowledge of God; 3) every thought that is not captive to the obedience of Christ.

The battlefield is in the mind. Satan battles for the control of our minds. Ideas have a spiritual dimension and as such exercise spiritual clout. We may not realise that ideas do affect us, but that does not prevent the ideas from having a profound effect in shaping our lives.

For example: if we get into the mentality that we are tired, and needing a break, then we can be pretty sure that we will feel tired and need a break. If, however, we are suddenly given the opportunity of doing something we have wanted to do for some time, it is amazing the effect this can have on us! How we think about any given thing will profoundly affect the level of energy that we have to put into that thing.

We have seen above that there are three main areas in which our minds are used to attack the things of God. We need to look at each of these in turn.

Speculation

From its beginning in the garden of Eden, the human race has been involved in speculating about virtually everything under the sun. This inquisitive side of our nature seems to be both good and bad, Yet we do not know how to confine our thoughts only to those areas that will have beneficial effects.

Satan's first question to the woman was, 'Has God said?' He knew perfectly well what God had said, but it was to his advantage to get her to question as much as possible. Who wants to take something as true just because the Lord has said it? Don't we need to prove things to our own satisfaction?

This same reasoning is behind much of what we now find difficult to understand or to believe in Scripture. The Lord may show us a course of action that to our way of thinking is really quite unreasonable. We, as rational creatures, feel that we have a right to understand before we are expected to act.

'But why should I?' is not just a question that our children ask when they are growing up. It is really much the same question that we all ask when we feel that God is demanding of us something that we do not want to give to Him.

The story of Naaman, as told in 2 Kings, chapter 3, is very instructive. Naaman was in the questioning attitude of mind mentioned above when Elisha offered him the cure for his leprosy. Naaman was sure that his own ways would be just as good, even though he had already tried them, no doubt, and found that they did not work!

Are we any different from that? It seems that almost anything, rather than the cross, will do for us to find release from our sin and guilt. Our speculations are virtually always against God. How slow we are to take Him or His word at face value!

I well remember the young girl who lived on a hippy commune near our first practice. She came in to see me with a variety of minor anxieties and pressures that were affecting her life. As we began to talk together it was obvious that the only real answer to her needs would be found in Jesus. This was very new ground to her and she was quite excited by it. I encouraged her to come to a meeting in our home that evening.

She did come to the meeting and at the gathering she found the new life that she was looking for. However, what amazed me was the reaction of her friends when she told them that she was coming to a Christian meeting. They were all incredulous that she would even consider such a possibility as having any answers for life. Some suggested that she might like to go to our local Buddhist centre. Another suggested that she might try Transcendental Meditation. A further one suggested that she should just get some more 'pot'.

Many speculations - and all raised up actively against the knowledge of the one true and living God. We do well to remember what we are taught in Romans 14:23, 'Whatever is not from faith is sin'. Our questioning rarely, if ever, leads us into a deeper awareness of the Lord. Much more commonly it becomes the ground on which we decide that we cannot trust the Lord in this matter.

Much of modern theology seems to rest on raising as many questions as it can about the word of God. We now have bishops - even a majority of them if the polls in the newspapers are to be believed - who speculate as to whether or not Jesus was really raised from the dead. Presumably even fewer of them really expect Him to return bodily as is so clearly promised in the Bible.

Our *belief* does not change the truth one little bit. It may change our personal experience of that truth, but God's truth stands whatever our reaction to it. Our attitude to the Bible as the word of God is going to have a profound influence on how we come to counsel people. We need to see it as *the* textbook. Then, even at times when we find it hard to believe that the Bible approach will help a person, we can still act in faith, expecting to see God work.

An old saying about the Bible that I heard as a child stated,

'God said it,
I believe it,
That settles it.'

I heard this restated recently, leaving out one small portion, in a way that I feel well illustrates what I have been saying.

'God said it,
That settles it.'

We need to learn to trust what God says and not merely to speculate about it.

Lofty Imaginations

Even as Satan fed the first speculations into the human mind, so he taught us how to use our God-given imagination against the Lord.

'You shall be as God.' Imagine that! No more of someone else higher up the totem pole telling you what to do. 'You will know all about good and evil' (Gen. 3:1-5).

We basically think of ourselves and our situations as if God is not around. This is the lofty imagination that is here spoken of. And this applies to Christian and non-Christian alike. By leaving God out of our reckoning, we inevitably run into problems that we do not know how to cope with. If only we admitted our utter dependence on Him! How secure we could then feel, knowing that 'Dad' will take care of everything!

Imagination is a powerful tool. We can use it for much good or for much evil. Tragically, we have used it mainly for evil. People fill their minds with such things as horror films, and then imagine all sorts of terrors behind every dark corner. No wonder fear grips them at times!

When we do let our imaginations come under the control of the Holy Spirit, we find that they are powerful creative tools in the hand of God. Dr Paul Yongghi Cho helped the Church at large see what can happen when a group of people allow their imagination to reach out after a powerful manifestation of the presence of God. With his church now over the 500,000 mark, it is hard not to believe that 'all things are possible to him who believes' (Mk. 9:23).

Often, in trying to help people to overcome the problems that they encounter, we will want to teach them how to use their imagination constructively. One of my favourite verses in this context is Ephesians 3:20, 'Now to Him who is able to do exceeding abundantly beyond all that we ask or think, according to the power that works within us. . .'.

Imagining ourselves as whole, well people is a very valuable tool to help us to get back into a position of wholeness, when we feel damaged.

Every Thought

Only the Bible could give us such an impossibly high standard as to 'bring every thought captive to Christ'. Were it not for the working of the Holy Spirit in us, I think that most of us would find that our thoughts give us a hard time.

Very early on in the Scriptures we find the Lord commenting on how corrupt our thoughts naturally are. 'Then the Lord saw that the wickedness of man was great on the earth, and that every intent of the thoughts of his heart was only evil continually' (Gen. 6:5).

Jesus, in commenting on how our heart naturally thinks, put things in a similar way, 'For out of the heart come evil thoughts. . .' (Mt. 15:19). We may like to believe that we naturally think about God, but unfortunately, this is just not true. Anyone who has tried to discipline their mind to think about God knows how easily we become distracted.

Just reflect on the last time you intended to spend some time praying. As soon as you get down to it you think of the letter that you were supposed to write yesterday. You make a note of it so that you will not be distracted. Then you try to pray again. You remember that you have not phoned someone that you had promised you would contact today. You phone the person, and then get back to prayer. You have hardly begun when you think to yourself, 'I will just read a chapter of the book beside the bed'. You pick it up, realise what you have done and put it down again! Again you begin to pray. Suddenly your mind is filled with all sorts of horrible images. Where on earth did those thoughts come from? And so the battle continues.

Any who have begun on the path of bringing their thoughts and prayers truly under the hand of God will have experienced something like this. The great joy is that we can persevere - and win. Since we have come to Christ we can discover the joy of knowing that we 'have the mind of Christ' (1 Cor. 2:16).

As we allow the very thoughts of God to penetrate into our being, we find that they work within us to make us whole. Meditating on the word of God is one effective way of doing this.

'Thy word I have treasured in my heart,
That I might not sin against Thee' (Ps. 119:11).

'The unfolding of Thy words gives light;
It gives understanding to the simple' (Ps. 119:130).

Mrs Jean Darnall, the well-known evangelist, taught many of us who went to Christian Life College a valuable way of applying this truth. If people came for counsel she would leave them with a few verses that they should 'take three times a day'. Each time they should read each of the verses out loud three times, first to themselves, then to the devil, and then to the Lord!

I have often used the same tool to help others and have found it invaluable. Many believers who are helped by the Lord find this an easy and effective way of fighting back against the enemy when he tries to take away from them what the Lord has done.

Whatever captures our mind will end up capturing us! The way that we think is profoundly important. The great battles for human minds are not between communism and capitalism, or between hedonism and pragmatism, but between belief in God as revealed in Christ and humanism. The choice now, as always, is clear. Do we think as God has taught us to think in His word, or do we choose to go to the tree of the knowledge of good and evil? One way leads inevitably to life; the other equally inevitably leads to death.

In the New Testament we are urged to be careful 'lest as the serpent deceived Eve by his craftiness, your minds should be led astray from the simplicity and purity (of devotion) to Christ' (2 Cor. 11:3). For most of us this temptation away from simplicity is a very great one. It seems that the more that we have learned of human wisdom, the more difficult we find it truly to believe the Lord. I can well remember George Tarleton saying in the early days of the charismatic movement, 'the church is dying by degrees; BAs, MAs, and even PhDs abound - but where is the power of God?'

I frequently find that my knowledge of medicine actually makes it more difficult to pray with people for them to be set free by the power of Christ. Slowly I am beginning to have a confidence in His power to free people of the emotional and mental or even demonic bondages that hold them. More difficult for me is having faith in His miraculous power in the physical realm. Some people find that this works the other way around. What I know is that I want to move freely in releasing the power of God in every area where people hurt!

We are held back from seeing this power of God because Satan has bewitched us even as he did Eve in the garden. We have been captured by 'philosophy and empty deception, according to the tradition of men, according to the elementary principles of the world, rather than according to Christ' (Col. 2:8). Humanism, in one of its many forms, traps us into thinking along the lines of human thought, rather than God's word. Western, scientific thought insists that everything can be observed, repeated and then 'proved'. But we cannot put God into our boxes and categories.

'The wind blows where it wishes and you hear the sound of it, but do not know where it comes from and where it is going; so is everyone who is born of the Spirit' (Jn. 3:8). We can no more easily keep track of God than we could try to hold the wind in our hands. We see His effects, but we do not see Him. 'Unless one is born again, he cannot see the kingdom of God', Jesus told Nicodemus in a later part of the passage quoted above.

We may not realise it, but the 'philosophies and . . . traditions of men' mentioned in Colossians 2:8 are actually demonically inspired. The 'elementary principles of the world' are demonic beings whose role it is, in the spiritual warfare that is constantly raging, to capture our minds. It is these same 'principalities' that are referred to in Ephesians 6:12: 'for our struggle is not against flesh and blood, but against principalities and powers'.

Ideas do not have to be obviously evil before they can come out of the pit of hell! Satan delights in transforming himself into an angel of light. He will take any guise, however respectable, if by it he can keep us in darkness. And in darkness we will stay until we let the 'light of the knowledge of the glory of God in the face of Christ' shine upon us.

A simple example may help to reinforce some of these concepts. A young woman in our fellowship called my wife and me out to see her one evening because she was apparently having a miscarriage. This had happened to her on seven previous occasions! Only her first child had gone to full term and he had died shortly after birth. Obviously any pregnancy was going to be very precious.

We had been praying on our way to the friend's home. As we talked together it became clear that this was actually a spirit of miscarriage that had found a way to attack our friend. We knew that we must tell her something of what the Lord had revealed to us.

I was having to deal with all sorts of doubts in my own mind. Thoughts like the following were pushing in: 'There are very good reasons why some people have recurrent miscarriages; maybe she has a hormonal problem; maybe the neck of the womb is too loose and she should have a stitch put through it to help support the developing baby.'

However, the Lord was saying to us that the problem was demonically inspired. And now some of those demons' companions were working on my mind to keep me trapped in my medical way of thinking and unable to receive the impressions that the Holy Spirit was giving.

We did pray for her. We commanded the spirit to leave in the name of Jesus. Our friend's lovely little girl is now 18 months old, and she has just had another child. Isn't the Lord good when we do take our courage in our hands and learn to rely on the truthfulness of His word to us?

The human mind is wonderfully complex and powerful. It is also the primary sphere in which we experience the attacks of Satan. It is little wonder then that so many people, be they Christians or as yet unbelievers, need help in sorting out their minds.

In the autumn of 1984, the Rev John Wimber, of the Vineyard Christian Fellowship in California, came to London. The teaching that he gave at Central Hall, Westminster, focused on our need to expect the supernatural. The many manifestations of the presence and power of God served wonderfully to reinforce this point.

How did John Wimber manage to take a large group of Western, well-educated, mainly scientifically trained people, and bring them to an expectation of the supernatural? The answer is found in the 'world-view' that he kept encouraging us into. He helped us to see that we can look at all of life from a number of viewpoints. Western scientific humanism is only one of these. Most people in other cultures would tend to have a more 'spiritually' minded viewpoint that expects the supernatural. The Bible certainly starts from the presumption that as God is, He is free to do what He wants. He is free to break in upon our experience and manifest His supernatural power.

A short while ago in the surgery I had an experience that illustrates this question of how we choose to look at things.

A middle-aged West Indian patient came in to see me. She was pretty well known to me as she had been on minor tranquillisers for some time. On this occasion she was looking, if anything, more down than normal. I began to ask her a few questions to see if there was some way that I could help.

To my surprise she told me that she had recently begun to hear voices. In the few minutes that a typical surgery consultation consists of, I knew that I had little time to go into this. I could tackle it from one of two vantage points. I could start from the view that this was a mental manifestation of psychiatric disease. If this were to be my approach I would need to ask for other signs and symptoms that would help me to make a firm diagnosis. Because of the voices I would probably look for what are medically the other major criteria for establishing a diagnosis of schizophrenia.

However, another approach would be to consider the possibility that the problem was based in the realm of the spirit. This would mean asking totally different questions to try to find out the spiritual root. I opted in the little time that I had to use the latter approach.

A few questions later, a brief assessment of her own view of what was happening, and it became clear that the problem was almost certainly demonic. We were able to pray together in the name of Jesus, and she was wonderfully set free. In the six months between that time and writing this chapter, she has had no further symptoms to the best of my knowledge.

People are going to come to us with all sorts of different problems. They are obviously not all going to be either as clear or as dramatic as some of the examples that I have given so far. We do need to see that our own minds are being renewed. We need to let the Holy Spirit begin to reshape our basic assumptions (the world-view that we operate from), so that we operate from a Biblical basis in all of our counselling.

In a later chapter we are going to look more fully at some of the wonderful weapons that the Lord has given us both to renew our minds and to fight off the attacks of the enemy. Truly we are 'taking every thought captive to the obedience of Christ' (2 Cor. 10:50).

6: Satan's Attack

'For our struggle is not against flesh and blood, but against the rulers, against the world forces of this darkness, against the spiritual forces of wickedness in the heavenly places. Therefore take up the full armour of God' (Eph. 6:12-13).

'Flesh and blood did not reveal this to you, but My Father who is in heaven' (Mt. 16:17).

'(I pray) that the God of our Lord Jesus Christ, the Father of Glory, may give to you a spirit of wisdom and of revelation in the knowledge of Him. I pray that the eyes of your heart may be enlightened' (Eph. 1:17-18).

Sir Tom Lees, who with his wife, Faith, opened up their family home for it to become the Post Green Community, used to lecture at Christian Life College. I can well remember his saying, 'You need spiritual eyes to spiritualise the Bible'.

Nowhere does this become more apparent than when we begin to look at the question of spiritual warfare. Considering how unreal the realm of the spirit is to many Christians, it is hardly surprising that we know as little as we do about prayer and other types of warfare. I can remember how shocked and outraged I was when I began to see some of the ways that Satan has of fighting against God's people.

Satan does not ever play fair. We need to realise that he is 'our adversary, the devil'. He is in this for all time. He knows that he has lost, but is too proud ever to give up. So he wants to make sure that he takes as many down with him as possible when he goes. The is nothing gentlemanly or clean about the way that Satan fights. We must assume that all of his tactics will be dirty. He delights in hitting below the belt!

We see this very clearly in the way that he attacks people's minds and emotions. Evil (negative) spirits do have access to our minds and can affect them. We must learn how we can fight back. We need to have our defences up so that we can ward off attack in the first place.

We do ourselves and the enemy an injustice if we underestimate the power of this attack. There may not be devils around every corner, but there are plenty that will find a way to hit out at us when we are least expecting it.

Dr Peter Quinton, a Christian GP, who is also a well-known conference speaker and teacher, has helpfully outlined the following ways that we find ourselves under attack by Satan and his demons: Sin, Surprise, Seige, Subtlety, Seance (the occult).

Sin

The Bible warns us 'not to be ignorant of (Satan's) schemes' (2 Cor. 2:11). Sin will inevitably 'give the devil an opportunity' (Eph. 4:27).
One of the commonest ways that we sin is in our unwillingness to forgive each other. How quickly we move into bitterness and resentment! It was this very sin that Paul was referring to in 2 Corinthians 2:11 when warning us to watch out for Satan's attacks. The Lord Jesus taught us to pray, 'Forgive us our debts, as we also have forgiven our debtors' (Mat. 6:12)

Sin provides, as it were, a small chink in our armour. The

more frequently that we give in to a particular sin, the wider that chink becomes. In the end the devil would be able to hit us with his fiery darts even with his eyes closed!

A few years ago I had an experience that shows how quickly and how effectively Satan can hit out at us. For some time I had known that I had the tendency to tell 'little white lies' to protect myself when the need arose. My conscience was too delicate to tell out-and-out lies, but making the edges grey so as to put me into a better light seemed to be OK!

Life had been getting very pressurised at home, particularly because of the frequency with which our phone was ringing. So we decided to buy a telephone answering machine. I phoned around a few companies, and then settled on one which seemed to be the best in our price range. Having agreed on the sale over the phone, I then discovered to my horror a couple of days later that I could buy the identical machine at two thirds of the price that I had agreed on with the first firm. Not wanting to be 'done' out of about £60, I decided to cancel my previous order by stating that I had 'changed my mind' about having a machine. The only trouble was that this was not the truth.

At the end of that week I had a large conference where we were expecting in the region of 500 professional people from all over the country. The subject of my talk was to be 'They Exchanged the Truth for a Lie'. Every time I settled down to try to prepare the talk a little voice would whisper to me, 'How can you teach other people about this when you are such a liar yourself?'

I knew this was the truth, but I also knew that it was not the Lord who was accusing me. How should I handle it? For several days I battled in my mind. Finally I gave in. If I was to hear the Lord give me something to say at the conference I knew I would have to settle this once and for all.

With much hesitation, I phoned up the original shop, and explained that I had not been honest with them, and would be happy to go ahead with the order if that was what they wanted. They eventually kindly agreed to cancel the order, and just charge me an administrative charge for their time involved. Twenty pounds poorer, and a whole lot wiser, I settled back to work on the talk for the weekend. When the conference came, I found that the Lord was manifesting great power. How glad I was that I had finally dealt with my sin!

As the Lord said to Cain when he became angry at God for not accepting his offering, 'If you do well, will not your countenance be lifted up? And if you do not well, sin is crouching at the door; and its desire is for you, but you must master it' (Gen. 4:7).

And master it we can. Christ has made the perfect provision for us. 'Sin shall not have dominion over you' (Rom. 6:14), is the promise made to us. With this assurance, we do not need to fear that Satan will always find some way through our sin to attack us. Rather we can trust the Lord to keep us free from all taint of sin.

Surprise

Anything that comes upon us suddenly has the capacity to frighten us. Sometimes this is pleasurable. How many of us have hidden behind a corner and then 'caught' our child into our arms unexpectedly as they come around the corner? The squeals of delight let us know how much it was enjoyed.

However, the same scene becomes terrifying if we just picture the arms that grab us belonging to someone whom we do not know, and that person placing a hand over our mouth to prevent us screaming. Whose hands it is makes all of the difference.

'Do not be afraid of sudden fear,
Nor of the onslaught of the wicked when it comes;
For the Lord will be your confidence,
And will keep your foot from being caught' (Prov.
3:25-26).

We cannot help, in most instances, the things that come upon us suddenly. What we can do is to learn to guard our hearts from a wrong reaction. Solomon was describing us well when he said, 'Moreover, man does not know his time; like a fish caught in a treacherous net, and birds trapped in a snare, so the sons of men are ensnared at an evil time, when it suddenly falls on them' (Eccles. 9:12).

When we are caught off guard, we are likely to be especially vulnerable. A number of years ago, some ministers who were all taking an active leading role in the developing Charismatic Movement got together for the morning. They had had a lovely time of friendship and fellowship. As they gathered to say their goodbyes outside the home where they had met, there was a car accident right outside the house. Rather shocked, they rushed over to help. Fortunately no-one had been seriously hurt.

A couple of weeks later, one of them noticed that he was feeling rather down in the dumps. He phoned up the person whose home they had met in. To his surprise this friend was also feeling rather low. They phoned around some of the others and found that since they had spent their morning together most of them had been feeling rather oppressed. In talking this over they realised that since seeing the car crash, they had all felt very vulnerable. The enemy had caught them off guard, and thrown some 'fiery darts' at them. The darts had found their mark.

Now that they saw the root, they were able to pray against it. Over the phone they prayed for each other, and were set free.

Seige

It may not have occurred to us that Satan delights to 'wear down the saints of the Highest One' (Dan. 7:25). There is a place for weariness or even exhaustion in the work of the Lord. We should not be afraid of hard work or lack of sleep at times. But during these times we do become especially vulnerable.

One of Satan's favourite tricks is to bring us under 'seige' by placing people in need of deliverance in our path round about 11pm! It has been a long day, and you are ready for bed. The doorbell rings, and one of your brothers in the church has brought round the person who has been causing so much trouble in their home group.

'(X) says that he will let us pray for him now', says your friend.

This may be the time to say, 'Well, the problem has kept until this moment. I suggest that you come back tomorrow about 7pm and we can then all pray about things together. We will all feel much fresher that way!'

My own experience has also shown that it is seldom wise to spend a long time in lengthy deliverance sessions. I remember one occasion when I had arranged to see a young man two hours before an important meeting began. He had become heavily demonised by an active involvement in the occult background to the martial arts in which he was an expert.

We started to pray, and a number of demonic beings began to show themselves. Things were going fine until we reached the spirit who seemed to be the king-pin among them. We just could not set this young man free. Finally I told the demon, 'You either come out right now or else I am going to take this young man into the big meeting with me.' I told the demon that if I did this then he would have to let go of his hold on this man in the meeting and many more people would see the power of Jesus and the humiliation of this demon. With a mighty shriek, the demon left, and the young man was free!

When you minister in the name of Jesus, and under His blood, you are in charge and so you should call the tune. Don't let the enemy boss you around.

Subtlety

The Nine o'clock News has just finished. The evening film comes on and seems to be pretty harmless. You are just getting into the plot, when it begins to turn a bit nasty. As you are tired, you decide just to watch a little bit more to see if it improves. Before you know where you are you have seen the whole film, your planned time with the Lord has gone out of the window, and to make it worse, you feel pretty awful inside.

What has happened? In an unguarded moment the enemy has slipped in and left you with the feeling of a cloud over your life.

My wife and a friend were spending some time in praying together as they did most weeks. The friend confided that she was feeling pretty down and depressed, but for no obvious cause. The two of them prayed together and asked the Lord to bring a real freedom and joy back, which He did in a wonderful way.

Later in the week, when the friend was again spending some time in prayer, the Lord told her that the source of the previous depression had been through reading the local paper that week. It had been full of murder and violence of other types, and had made her vulnerable in the unguarded way that she had read it. She knew that she needed to be more careful in the future to follow the Biblical pattern of letting your mind dwell only on 'whatever is honourable, whatever is right, whatever is pure, whatever is lovely, whatever is of good repute . . .' (Phil. 4:8).

Unguarded relationships can themselves be the cause of problems in this area. Some Christians belong to secret societies like the Freemasons. While in some circles this is still a matter for debate, for those who take the word of God seriously, this is, and always has been, a taboo area.

'If your brother, your mother's son, . . . entices you secretly saying, "Let us go and serve other gods" (whom neither you nor your fathers have known), you shall not yield to him or listen to him' (Deut. 13:6).

'I am the Lord, and there is none else.
I have not spoken in secret,
In some dark land' (Is. 45:19).

'But we have renounced the things hidden because of shame, not walking in craftiness or adulterating the word of God, but by the manifestation of truth commending ourselves to every man's conscience in the sight of God' (2 Cor. 4:2).

These, and other similar verses help us to see that we need to walk in open declaration of the truth of God. The word of God specifically forbids us to be joined in close association with others who are not believers. Secret societies directly contravene this command of the Lord, and as such tend to open their participants up to further attack from the enemy.

Of course, one reason that they remain secret is that we will not know what goes on. Jesus said that 'men loved the darkness rather than the light, for their deeds were evil' (Jn. 3:19).

Seance (Occult)

This fifth area could just as easily have been listed under

'sin', but it is such an important means of enemy attack that it is probably best to devote a little space to it on its own.

Most spirit-filled Christians are now aware that all contact with the occult is forbidden to the Christian. The danger of these contacts, even the most casual of them, is shown in the following situation.

A doctor friend of ours related the following to me. One day while at school, she had gone with another Christian friend to a gathering of some of their classmates. They had gone to see what they were up to, not in any sense to participate in anything wrong. The 'meeting' turned out to be a seance.

They had not been there very long when they both got rather frightened and left. My friend commented that following this experience (though she in no way linked it to the seance at the time) she had a very difficult first term at university; she found it difficult to get through to God, and she lost much of the confidence in the Lord that she had previously had.

We prayed very simply that any negative effect of that experience should be broken, and that she should be free to go on in the Lord.

Two weeks later I saw her again. She now told me that she could hardly believe how much her life had changed. She had not realised it, but in all sorts of ways she had previously been oppressed by the devil. It was not until the cloud was lifted as we prayed that she realised just how oppressed she had been. It was now glorious to be truly free.

If such an encounter by a young believer could lead to problems, how much more the deliberate involvement in occult practices that many still take part in! The reading of horoscopes is not a joking affair. We may pretend that we do not pay any attention to them, but the only way to be sure is not to read them in the first place!

Many Christians like reading books about the occult, or watching the late night horror films. Both of these avenues open us right up to enemy attack. If we have been involved in any of these things then we need to renounce them, and ask the Lord to free us from any effect that they may have had on us. Usually it is also wise to ask someone else to pray with us against the effects of these occult encounters.

Some years ago, when the film, *The Exorcist,* was being shown around the country, many Christians found themselves needing to counsel people whose lives were obviously coming under oppression since seeing the film. In some areas, like Plymouth, counselling organisations such as Crossline were set up to help with the large number of people who were coming to local Christians needing help. It is quite clear that even the watching of occult material in films can open a person's life to demonic attack.

Recently there has been a certain amount of material published in the medical press showing that growing numbers of psychiatrists, not all of them Christians, are becoming very unhappy at the effect of large doses of violence and occult films on their young viewers. Research in the United States has been so conclusive that the President's Commission on Television Viewing has recommended a drastic cut in the amount of violence shown on television.

Having seen a little of the ways in which the enemy will seek to attack us, let us look at some of the ways we can learn to fight back. These weapons will form our basic armoury as we seek to counsel others in their attack against Satan.

7: Our Weapons

'Let the high praises of God be in their mouth,
And a two-edged sword in their hand,
To execute vengeance on the nations,
And punishment on the peoples;
To bind their kings with chains,
And their nobles with fetters of iron;
To execute on them the judgement written;
This is an honour for all His godly ones.
Praise the Lord!' (Ps.149:6-9).

The weapons that the Lord has given us to fight back against Satan are wonderful. As we might expect of the Lord, using His weapons is not only a joy, but they also bring their own rich dividends into our lives. We can use praise as a weapon, but as a side effect it brings us into the presence of the Lord. Show me any traditional medicines that have that type of side effect!

Christians were made to be soldiers. As good soldiers we want to know what our weapons are and how to use them effectively. In my medical and pastoral work I have had many interesting opportunities to learn in this area.

Praise

Praise is, to me, the primary resource that we have seen the

Holy Spirit bring back to the body of Christ through the Charismatic Movement. 'All over the world the Spirit is moving', and all over the world people have begun to use praise in their worship.

We were created to praise. The book of Ephesians is full of the fact that God made us for praise. Three times in the first chapter it tells us that we were created 'to the praise of His glory' (Eph. 1:6,12,14).

Praise brings us into the presence of God. King David could say 'I will bless the Lord at all times, His praise shall continually be in my mouth' (Ps. 34:1). Did this not open him up to be able also to say, 'I have set the Lord continually before me; Because He is at my right hand, I will not be shaken.'?

This is a position of secure confidence. This is a position where we feel safe and Satan feels very vulnerable. Satan cannot cope with praise. Perhaps this is why he hates praise so much and will do anything to stop Christians from praising the Lord.

In praise we live in God's presence. In God's presence there is 'fulness of joy; In thy right hand there are pleasures forever' (Ps. 16:11). We can live on top. We do not have to spend all, or even most of our time under a cloud when we can be 'living under the shadow of His wings'.

The problem for us is not that we cannot praise God in any and every circumstance, but that we will not. 'How often I wanted to gather your children together, the way a hen gathers her chicks under her wings, and you were unwilling. Behold, your house is being left to you desolate!' (Mt. 23:37-38). The simple command of Scripture is that we are to 'rejoice' in the Lord always; again I will say, rejoice!' (Phil. 4:4). Or, as it is stated elsewhere in equally clear terms, 'Rejoice always; pray without ceasing; in everything give thanks; for this is God's will for you in Christ Jesus' (1 Thess. 5:16-18).

The capacity for us, or for those whom we counsel, to

overcome problems and pressures is already there. We need to live by the word of God.

I well remember the summer that I spent working in a Christian camp in the northern part of New York State. My work was rather inglorious. I washed up the dishes for about 130 people after each meal. If time permitted, I was then also responsible for helping with some of the meal preparation.

On one occasion the other young man who was due to be helping me had slipped out to see some friends who were just arriving by coach. I was feeling pretty low and tired. The day had begun, as each day at camp did, at 6.45am. I was just beginning to grumble and complain about my lot when the Lord reminded me that I could choose to live in praise.

I began praising the Lord and singing in the, by now, empty kitchen. After about ten minutes, unnoticed by me, the driver of the coach came in. I continued singing away and praising the Lord. Then I heard him call from somewhere in the kitchen, 'What are you so happy about? You seem to be the only one working around here.'

We quickly fell into conversation and I was able to tell him how the Lord is able to keep us in praise and in joy. As we talked together, the presence of God enveloped me in such a sweet way. God had more than compensated me for any supposed injustice in my having to continue to work.

From down in the deepest depths, the sudden awareness of the presence of God is enough to bring us back into the joy of the Holy Spirit. Some see praise as an easy way out. They should try it! I know of no more effective way of bringing the cross of Christ into our lives. As we praise God, whatever is happening around us, we push our own desires down, and see ourselves as utterly dependent on God. This is the very place that we, as created beings, ought to be.

Praise, though, goes much farther in its effects. It not only brings us into the presence of God. It actively hits out against the enemy.

Merlin Carothers, the author of *Prison to Praise* and many other books, tells the following story.

At the beginning of most of their services, his church had slipped into the habit of binding all of the spirits that were in the place. It seemed that they had to go through this ritual of 'binding the spirits' before the sense of heaviness would leave the meetings and they felt free to move on in praise and worship. And so each meeting began with this 'fighting' against the enemy.

One day the Lord said to Merlin as he was preparing, 'You know, the demons from all around this area come to be at the start of your meetings. They all love the show when you give them the credit for holding the meeting down. Tonight you are not to bind the enemy, but just to move out in praise.'

Merlin acted on what the Lord had told him. They had a tremendous time. Right from the start they were able to worship in the presence and power of God.

Praise is a formidable weapon. Satan cannot stand up to praise. When King Jehoshaphat sent out the musicians and praisers ahead of his army, the enemy were defeated! 'And when they began singing and praising, the Lord set ambushes against the sons of Ammon, Moab, and Mount Seir, who had come against Judah; so they were routed' (2 Chron. 20:21-22). It was the same principle in operation at Jericho.

I was at a small conference back in 1980 that was attended mainly by medical people from around the country. We were a mixture of consultants, GPs, those in the early part of their postgraduate training, and a few who were not connected with the medical profession at all.

On the Sunday morning the Lord directed us to spend some time in prayer. He had showed us that we were to dedicate this portion of the conference to prayer for the needs of others outside our own group and that this would release His blessing to us. We began to pray particularly for those who were involved with working in prisons. The Lord showed us that we were to stand up and march around the room, even as they had marched around Jericho. Then we were to shout His victory over this area of needy people.

Can you imagine it as this apparently select group of people began to march in a most undignified way around the conference room? Anyone looking on at that point would have been ready to have all of us certified! But God began to move. As we began to express 'high praises' we knew that something had been broken down in the prison world that would result in many prisoners coming to Christ. More immediately apparent was the breaking down that was already going on in us. We certainly did see a release of all that the Lord was wanting to say to us.

Vigorous, vocal, extended times of praise are tremendously releasing. Sometimes in meetings where the Holy Spirit is allowed to lead the people, you will find many set free just by the praise. On a number of occasions, I have seen the hardest people, Christian or non-Christian, melted by the presence of God in praise and brought to repentance and tears.

Many people that I have counselled have been most resistant to the Lord doing anything in their lives. I have tried to help them see the root of their need. I have shown them areas where they may not be living in accordance with the word of God. They may agree with all of this, and still not see any improvement. Then I encourage them to praise. It seems as if any cure rather than praise would be preferred! With reluctance they agree to try what God has asked of them. As they begin falteringly to praise they find to their surprise an almost immediate release. Praise confounds the enemy, brings in the presence of God, and releases us into our high calling in God.

Prayer and Fasting

All of us who are believers agree that we should pray. Most of us know such verses as, 'All things for which you pray and ask, believe that you have received them, and they shall be granted you' (Mk. 11:24).

The truth is, though, that we find it difficult to pray. We find it even more difficult to fast and pray. It was reading Dr Paul Bilheimer's excellent little book, *Destined For the Throne*, that began to open me up to the limitless possibilities that are ours when we learn to pray. The Lord has created us to reign with Him. We are not just passive people on our way to heaven. We are soldiers who, even now, are being trained to reign with Christ, through the medium of prayer. We can effectively extend the Kingdom of God by our participation through prayer. Prayer is not us trying to force God's hand into doing what He does not want to do. In prayer we learn to marshall our thoughts and desires in line with the thoughts and desires of the Holy Spirit. When we are praying in harmony with the will of God, then He both hears and answers our praying (1 Jn. 5:14-15). Prayer does not change God's mind, it changes ours!

Intercession is the privilege of every believer. The prophet Isaiah expresses God's surprise when he writes, 'And He saw that there was no man, and was astonished that there was no-one to intercede' (Is. 59:16). It is not that God cannot act without us, but He has chosen to limit His actions in such a way that we can learn to participate in His Kingdom rule. As we pray, we are learning to reign with Christ.

To say that we reign with Christ in prayer, though, is also to admit that when we do not pray the kingdom of darkness is free to advance. It is not that the Lord could not prevent this advance, but that we would not learn to fight if the Lord did not involve us in real battles. Sadly we often learn more through our errors than we do through our successes. That the Lord should be willing to tie the progress of the Kingdom of God to our attempts at learning to pray is to me quite astounding.

Some years ago now Felicity and I went out to Korea to see Dr Paul Yongghi Cho's church. We had heard much about it, and I had been profoundly challenged and changed by his book, *The Fourth Dimension*. We had, at that time, been going through a difficult time in our own lives and in the church of which we were a part.

As we met with different people in Korea we began to quiz them as to how they would deal with the needs that we personally experienced and encountered in others. The answer seemed always to be that 'we should fast and pray'.

They did not plan lengthy counselling sessions. They did not go round from one person to another until they heard the answer that they wanted. They fasted and prayed. And what results they received!

As we humble ourselves in fasting, we see the hand of the Lord released to do some amazing things. Over recent times in our church we have seen a growing number of people set free from long-standing problems by prayer and fasting. 'This kind does not go out except by prayer and fasting'

(Mt. 17-21) is not only the experience of the disciples of Jesus. In our counselling we will often find situations where we seem to hit a brick wall until we begin to fast and pray. I think that this is one reason why Satan does whatever he can to hinder Christians from learning to fast. Almost any excuse is usually enough to stop one from fasting. Dr Cho's mother-in-law, Jashil Choi, has written a most helpful book about fasting called *Korean Miracles*. It is an excellent starting place for any who are wanting to explore this area.

I don't know if any of us find it easy to learn to pray. Again and again I have set myself to the task of learning to go deeper in this area. I know that more of my friends would be saved if I learnt how to pray for them. I know that I would be more effective within my family and church if I prayed faithfully for them. But my knowing is not enough. I find the learning is actually very hard work.

The disciples were constantly challenged by all that they saw of Jesus' prayer life. No wonder they asked, 'Lord, teach us to pray.' But even they did not become prayer warriors overnight. At the end of Jesus' earthly ministry they were still able to fall asleep in prayer at a most crucial time, in the garden of Gethsemane. There is definitely still hope for us.

Prayer does change things. Each of us will find the truth of William Cowper's words:

> Satan trembles when he sees
> The weakest saint upon his knees.

Prayer warfare is freely available to all of us.

Spoken Confession of the Word of God

It is fascinating listening to what people say about themselves.

'I know that I won't be able to get this done in time.'

'Nobody really likes me. They only put up with me because they are Christians.'

'I don't suppose that the Lord will ever want to use me like that. I know that I couldn't give a message in tongues in our church.'

And so we go on, actually creating the negative environment that we are then going to have to live in. It is not surprising that we see so little happening around us.

The spoken word has tremendous effect. James said that the person who can control his tongue is 'a perfect man, able to bridle the whole body as well' (Js. 3:2). So much of what we hear people say is destructive. When Solomon lists the seven things which the Lord hates, no fewer than three of them are directly related to what we say (Prov. 6:16-19). 'Death and life are in the power of the tongue' (Prov. 18:21). We can help people choose life.

I know a young man who always comes out with a whole host of negatives when you ask him how he is. You almost feel afraid to ask. What new things has he found to feel mournful about today? What a contrast this is to people who can virtually always find something good to say about their situation and about others around them. This sort of person is a joy to be with.

Faith in God demands that we speak out about the goodness of the Lord. It also demands that we speak out specifically about the good things that He is doing for us right now in our present situation. 'But the righteousness based on faith *speaks* thus, "do not *say* in your heart 'Who will ascend into heaven?' (that is, to bring Christ down), or 'Who will descend into the abyss?' (that is to bring Christ up from the dead). But what does it *say*? The word is near you *in your mouth and in your heart (that is, the word of faith which we are preaching), that if you confess with your mouth*

Jesus as Lord and believe in your heart that God raised Him from the dead, you shall be saved' (Rom. 10:6-9, my italics).

When we choose to speak about what God has promised in a situation, we honour the Lord. When we stay silent, we are usually hiding our doubts! Our open declaration of what God is doing actually releases the life of God within us to see the deed done.

Words have creative power, 'God said', and it happened. 'He sent His word and healed them, and delivered them from their destructions' (Ps. 107:20). We should not underestimate what can happen when we speak in the name of the Lord.

Control of the tongue is vital. We must control what we say to people by way of counsel. All must learn to control what they say by way of personal confession. No wonder the Holy Spirit gives us the gift of tongues! We need to learn to yield our tongues to the Holy Spirit. Speaking out in a new tongue is a tremendous asset in learning how to do this.

James tells us to be 'quick to hear, slow to speak and slow to anger' (Jas. 1:19). Most of us could do with help to hear much more, and say much less. We should never forget when we find ourselves in the position of being asked for counsel, that people do not really want to hear from us; they want to hear from the Lord. What a wonderful and terrible responsibility this is! We do better to point the person right back to the Lord and listen with them, than to speak just from our own understanding.

Using the gift of tongues begins to shape our own understanding. We begin to be much less reliant on ourselves, and more dependent on what we hear the Holy Spirit saying to us. I find it fascinating that the apostle Paul, even from his position of maturity and intimacy with Jesus, could still say to the Corinthian Christians that, 'I thank God that I speak in tongues more than you all' (1 Cor. 14:18). My feeling is that this was an integral part of his maturity in Christ.

There has been a tendency in charismatic circles to play down the value of this precious gift from God. As if any gift of the Holy Spirit is 'least' in value! Satan has stirred up so much trouble and controversy over tongues just because it is so important. He has more idea than us of the power that there is in this gift of God. If God has given you this gift, then use it! If He hasn't given it to you, then ask for it!

No believer has to be without this gift. It is one of the sign gifts that are listed in Mark 16 as available to all believers. We do not have to feel that 'I am the one person that God does not want to give this gift to'. God does not have favourites. If we ask He gives 'to all men generously and without reproach. But let him ask in faith without any doubting, for the one who doubts is like the surf of the sea driven and tossed by the wind. For let not that man expect that he will receive anything from the Lord' (Jas. 1:5-6).

Some may well ask, 'But what about 1 Corinthians 12 where it seems clearly to imply that not all have the gift of tongues, any more than all are apostles, or than all have the gift of the working of miracles?'

I used to puzzle over this myself, as I knew from other Scriptures that tongues was available to us all. In discussing this with others, I saw that this passage in 1 Corinthians 12 is not talking about the personal use of this gift of tongues, but rather of its public or church use. Here it is linked with the interpretation of tongues.

Certainly not all are gifted by the Holy Spirit to bring a public message for the church in tongues. But the personal use of the gift of tongues will build up the individual. The public use of the gift to bring a message from the Lord to a gathering of God's people will build up the Body. This latter usage of tongues, as with all of the other spiritual gifts, is not for personal edification so much as to bless and encourage the whole Body.

The very action of opening our mouths to speak makes us active participants by faith in this warfare. We can join in declaring the word of God. 'Death and life are in the power of the tongue,' declares Solomon. (Prov. 18:21). We are actively choosing life as we speak out our confident belief that God will do all that His word promises.

We see Jesus following this pattern when He was tempted by Satan in the wilderness, Whatever was thrown at Him, His reply was, 'It is written'. Similarly, as we learn the word of God, and then use it, we will find that it is a powerful 'two-edged sword' against the attacks of the devil (Heb. 4:12).

Forgiveness

In much the same way that our use of the tongue can profoundly affect both ourselves and others, so we see that our attitude towards others can do the same.

A woman came to my surgery with a long-standing problem of fears and depression. She virtually never went out of her house for fear that she would be mugged. I went to visit her one day in her home, and it took her several minutes to open the door as there were so many locks on it.

As we began to talk over her situation, it transpired that many years previously her brother had wronged her. She had never been able to forgive him for what he had done. In talking together, I was sure that this was at the root of her fears and insecurities. But she would not bring herself to forgive him. With great sadness I had to leave her, unable to pray with any confidence that God would set her free. The Bible is very clear: 'For if you forgive men for their transgressions, your heavenly Father will also forgive you. But if you do not forgive men, then your Father will not forgive your transgressions' (Mt. 6:14-15).

Unforgiveness in people's spirits is like a cloud that hangs over them, preventing the release of the Spirit in their life and ministry. I have seen this both in my own life and in the lives of others. We seriously weaken our attack on the enemy when we harbour any unforgiveness in our hearts towards others. Similarly we powerfully release the Spirit of God into a situation when we freely pass on the forgiveness which we have already received from Christ.

Many other weapons could be listed that the Lord has made available to us in our warfare. Faith is our shield against the enemy's attacks (Eph. 6:16), and our breastplate (1 Thess. 5:8) to complete our bodily armour. Weapons are offensive and defensive. We are ourselves weapons in the hand of our God (Jer. 51:20).

As we now begin to look at some of the specific areas where people so often come for counsel, let us ask the Lord to keep us mindful of our weapons which are 'divinely powerful for the destruction of fortresses'.

8: Depression

'Why are you in despair, O my soul, And why have you become disturbed within me? Hope in God, for I shall again praise Him' (Ps. 42:5).

Depression seems to be all around us. If joy is the 'flag flown high from the castle of the heart, when the King is in residence there,' then depression seems to be the signpost that we have moved out from the King's presence!

'In Thy presence there is fulness of joy' (Ps. 16:11). What are we to do with such Scriptures? Are we left saying that they only apply sometimes? Can we really live in this place of joy? Surely that is only for those with an even disposition and a naturally sunny temperament?

What about powerful workers for God, such as David Brainerd? He worked wonderfully in the revival among the North American Indians, yet he was described as very melancholy most of the time. Surely he was moving in God's presence?

Many other people who are known to us personally must come to mind. Is it an impossible dream to think that we can live free from this curse that seems to pervade Christendom along with the rest of the world? Yet as we read the Scriptures, our hearts hunger for more of the hope it brings.

'The Kingdom of God is not eating and drinking, but

righteousness and peace and joy in the Holy Spirit' (Rom. 14:17). It is not naïve to believe that we can take hold of such verses and see them as normal Christian experience. We are now a part of this Kingdom. Jesus has told us that 'the Kingdom of God is within you'.

But, for most, their experience is too strong for them to accept such statements with the simplicity of faith. 'Life is just not like that,' they say. Who says it isn't? 'Rather let God be found true, though every man be found a liar, as it is written, That Thou mightest be justified in Thy words, And mightest prevail when Thou are judged' (Rom. 3:4).

If it appears that our experience does not match up to the word of God, then we need to decide if we are going to fit God's word in with our experience, or whether we are going to find some way for our experience to be reshaped by the word of God.

Many times I have had people say to me, 'But it is easy for you, Tony, you never get depressed'. How do they know? We all get depressed. The question is not, 'Do you get depressed?', but rather, 'What do you do with your depression?' We need to learn to fight.

The joining of our will with the will of God is a vital part of our weaponry in counselling. How often we see in depression, in resentment, in guilt, in obesity, even in clear demonic oppression, that the pathway to freedom demands the full will of the person involved! We cannot absolve ourselves of our own responsibility for the situations that we find ourselves in.

It may be handy to blame circumstances, other people, hormones or even God. It may even be that any or all of these have had a major part to play in why we are now feeling like we do. But we still have a part to play ourselves.

Most people who have been involved in counselling over recent years will have become familiar with concepts involved in inner healing. The Holy Spirit has clearly brought to light many areas where we can pray to see people set free. However, some, in hiding behind things that have happened to them, or that have come down to them through their families, have failed to find lasting freedom. This is because they have been unwilling or unaware of their own need to carry the responsibility for their own problems. It is a clear principle of the new covenant that 'everyone will die for his own iniquity; each man who eats the sour grapes, his teeth will be set on edge' (Jer. 31:30).

Sometimes I wake up feeling rather down for no apparent reason. I may search my heart and find something there that is blocking my relationship with the Lord. Or I may look and not really find anything of substance. In either situation I have found that the Lord is well able to deal with it. Confession of any known sin is a necessary beginning. Then praise can quickly and powerfully bring us back into God's presence.

I used to have a house which was built on four storeys. In London space was always at a premium so I guess that they had to build upwards. It meant that the bedrooms were either two or three floors above the basement level. I used sometimes to go down into the basement before the others had woken and really shout my praise to God. These times of 'high praises' (Ps. 149:6) would powerfully deal with any sense of depression that was trying to oppress me.

We saw the Lord work similarly in Claire, who was a good friend of ours. She had recently come back to the Lord. She and her husband John were now an active part of the church where I was working as one of the leaders. They longed for their lives and their home to be truly available to the Lord, but they were finding this a real problem.

Every morning, Claire would wake up unaccountably depressed. This would be compounded if they were expecting any visitors during the day. She would worry about the meal. She would worry about the place settings. She would worry whether her cooking was up to the occasion. This worry and depression seemed to be dominating their lives.

In asking her if she knew why she reacted as she did, it came out that both her mother and her grandmother had tended to react in very similar ways. We agreed that we would pray and ask the Lord to set her free from this family tie which was holding her back from what the Lord had for her family.

A few weeks later, Claire casually remarked to me, 'It all seems to be all right now.' That was it. No heroics. No special praying. Nothing very dramatic at the time that we prayed. Just God stepping in and doing a miracle, and a young couple released to be what God wanted them to be. Now, many years later, they are constantly entertaining!

At different times we all come under pressure. Sometimes we can find a clear cause for this and sometimes we can't. Medically we would usually try to differentiate between these two primary ways in which depression shows itself.

If we can find a clear reason for the depression, then we tend to call it reactive, or exogenous (from outside) depression. Usually this is seen to be a self-limiting condition. Sometimes minor tranquillisers or, if necessary, antidepressants are used to help tide the sufferers over until they come out of the depression.

Endogenous (from inside) depression is usually viewed as depression that comes on without a clear cause. Many people experience times when they feel unaccountably depressed. Sometimes this proceeds from just the occasional off day to an extended period of time. For example, many women feel rather depressed in the few days following childbirth. Usually this quickly resolves itself.

However, for a small minority of women, the depression persists. Life seems to get blacker and blacker. They might blame this on the baby. They may feel that they cannot cope with a new child. Their marriage comes under increasing strain. The depression continues, and by now many doctors would have referred the woman for psychiatric help. Certainly she needs help of some kind.

Whether the medical classification of depression is really of any help is open to debate. I myself have real doubt as to whether there is such a thing as endogenous depression. Behind everything there must be a cause. Often we are still trying to find it! One reason that we may look for causes, and not find them, is that we are looking in the wrong places.

Jan had suffered from depression on and off for many years. She had been one of my patients for a time. I had tried to help her, but had not really been able to do so. On one occasion Jan had needed to be admitted to mental hospital for four months. No clear cause for her depression could be found. She had been given all the usual medications, but with no success.

One of the nurses who was working at the local psychiatric hospital had been talking to Jan about Jesus. She asked for, and received, permission to take Jan out one morning to church with her. At the end of the meeting she arranged for my wife to pray with Jan. Felicity first led Jan to committing her life to the Lord Jesus. Then they began to pray about Jan's depression.

As soon as they began to pray, Jan started to show signs of demonic problems. She began apparently to faint, to cry out, to struggle when someone tried to help her, etc. At this point my wife and the Christian nurse felt that it would be better to take Jan to our home for further help.

We took Jan home with us for lunch. I then phoned her

present GP, who is a lovely Christian doctor. He did not mind my continuing to pray for and minister to Jan.

Because we knew by now that Jan was under the influence of a demonic power which had held her bound for all these years, it was decided that I would pray with her while Felicity continued to look after the children. So I simply commanded the powers that were holding her to release her. In a very few minutes it was clear that she was free. We then talked over what it meant for her to follow Jesus with all of her heart. We subsequently prayed for her to be filled with the Holy Spirit.

This latter step of being filled with the Holy Spirit seems to me to be crucial. Jesus made it plain that after a spirit has left a person, it wanders around aimlessly looking for somewhere else to go. If it can't find anywhere, then it goes back to see if there is any chance of persecuting the same person again. If they have left their lives empty, the spirit may easily try to reinvade, but this time it may return with other 'friends'! We need to fi!! up all the space in our lives that we have reclaimed from the enemy with the presence of Jesus.

Jan was taken back to the psychiatric hospital at the end of the day. Her husband was so impressed with the changes in her over the next couple of weeks that he also gave his life to the Lord.

The hospital took a bit more convincing. However, within a couple of months they had her off her medication, and then discharged her. Her GP was as delighted as we were to see all that the Lord had done for Jan.

We never did find out what had been the original source of entry for this demonic power. What we do know is that demons always have to leave when Jesus tells them to go!

In passing, I feel I should mention that it is important that we are extremely careful to let other ministers or doctors know when we are trying to help someone they are already dealing with. Between doctors this is already demanded by professional codes of practice, let alone common courtesy. Between pastors and churches it is still wise, so that no-one feels that you are trying to 'steal their sheep'.

To try to understand all depressive episodes as having a specific demonic origin would be very naïve. We have many instances in Scripture of people who are obviously depressed. Sometimes the cause is plain; sometimes it isn't.

We are going to look at some sources of depression in the life of King David. He expressed himself and his emotions so clearly in the beautiful psalms that he has left us. As we look at these we are going to see several separate occasions when, for differing reasons, David found his own life under the cloud of depression.

Sin

David often found himself under pressure of his own making. Sometimes, as when his child by Bathsheba was very ill, it was clearly the hand of God dealing with him. It is interesting that in this worrying situation of having a child critically ill, he showed many of the classic symptoms of depression. He would not eat. He was withdrawn and moody. He was unable to sleep. Relief only came to David when He saw that the Lord would not change His mind about punishing him by allowing this child to die. Repentance had not brought relief. Only the finality of God dealing with the situation set David free. (See 2 Samuel 12 for this wonderfully revealing story.)

While it is probably pushing the point too far to take David's actions and ascribe them totally to depression, it is no mistake to recognise that we would probably have dealt with David very differently from the way the Holy Spirit dealt with him. David's sin had been severe. He had 'given occasion to the enemies of the Lord to blaspheme'. Because of this the Lord let him feel the weight of his sin.

Sin always has consequences. 'The wages of sin is death,' is as true now as when Paul first wrote it (Rom. 6:23). When we do things wrong, although the eternal consequences of those sins have already found their release in Jesus, the temporal consequences still need to be worked out in our experience.

I well remember when Pauline first came to see me. She was literally pushed in the door of my consulting room by the person who had brought her. The story that slowly emerged was tragic. She had four children. Two were living with her at present, and the other two were with her husband. He had left her some time ago because they were always fighting. She had been drinking quite a lot during that time, as had he.

When her husband left she had no way of supporting herself or the children - so she turned to prostitution. This life was so shaming and destroying her that she began to drink even more heavily. As she sobbed out this story, her final cry of despair was, 'I sometimes think that the only way out of this is suicide.'

Thoughts of suicide are very common in those who are depressed. Even attempts at suicide, usually little more than an impassioned plea for help, are disturbingly common. Tragically, some are going to succeed in their attempt.

To me, there is no real answer to a person who comes with Pauline's needs except in the Lord Jesus. Offering antidepressants to an alcoholic is just substituting one type of drug dependence for another. What do we offer to compensate for the loneliness of her husband having left her? Do we suggest, as some psychiatrists would nowadays, that she go out and have an affair to try to help her forget? She was doing that with a vengeance, and destroying herself in the process.

Sin, in the form of excessive alcohol, in the form of family breakdown, in the form of prostitution, was paying its deadly wage. The wages of sin is death. In this case the wages were a living hell.

The hymn-writer of old asked the question, 'What can take away my sin?' Back comes the answer, 'Nothing but the blood of Jesus.' That is still the truth, the whole truth, and nothing but the truth. We may try all sorts of pharmacological, psychological, or even philosophical answers. They will all be in vain. The only permanent answer to sin is the Lord Jesus and the forgiveness He offers.

Circumstantial Pressures

There were other times when King David's depression was not so much related to personal sin, as to a life under extreme pressure. The actual heading for Ps. 42 is, 'Thirsting for God in Trouble and Exile'.
'My tears have been my food day and night,
While they say to me all day long, 'Where is your God?'
These things I remember, and I pour out my soul within me.
For I used to go along with the throng and lead them in procession to the house of God,
With the voice of joy and thanksgiving, a multitude keeping festival.'

How often in depression we find ourselves looking backward. We remember the good old times, and everything seems even blacker in comparison. Our next question is the same as David's. 'Why are you in despair, O my soul? Why have you become disturbed within me?'

Tragically most of us do not get beyond the question. David did not remain in this attitude of self-pity. He did not go around asking everyone else why he was so down. He did not even get them to pray for him, as far as we can see. He responded to what he already knew of the workings of the Holy Spirit in him. He began to proclaim the word of the Lord to himself. Was this the first sign of madness? It may be so in some people's eyes, but it was David's salvation. His spoken word to himself set him free to 'hope in God'. The very word of encouragement became his word of release.

I don't doubt that it was as difficult for David to respond in this way to the prompting of the Holy Spirit as it is for us today. Who wants to be told to praise when all they feel like doing is having a moan? None of us like this. We can begin to see why, earlier on in this book, I suggested that the way of praise is the way of the cross. It cuts right across what we want, and moves us into a position of obedience to the word of God.

As David continues with this wonderful psalm that began in depression, but which is now beginning to progress to hope, we see the reality of his walk with God. He knows that God is going to see him through this rough patch. He is not pretending that he is not finding the going very rough, but neither is he just living in the pressure. He is declaring his clear and certain hope that God will bring him back into a position of joyful praise.

Middle Age Crisis

It is tremendously interesting to read many of the psalms, noting at what period of David's life they were written. Many of them are written during his middle years. He has done well. He is the ruler of the strongest empire on earth at the time, but his growing family are causing him a lot of headaches. He can control the world, but he does not know how to control his own family. He knows how to fight external enemies, but he is growing flabby against the enemy within.

It was 'at the time when kings go out to battle, that David sent Joab . . . But David stayed at Jerusalem. Now when evening came David arose from his bed and walked around on the roof of the king's house, and from the roof he saw a woman bathing; and the woman was very beautiful' (Sam. 11:1-2).

John is a successful doctor. He has three lovely children and a beautiful wife. He has been busy serving the Lord for a number of years, giving all of his free time to be available to all that is going on in his church where the Lord is doing some wonderful things. His marriage is good. But at the moment he and his wife are not really enjoying the sexual part of their relationship very much. There are also one or two other pressures on them. The children are growing up, and the middle child is getting very rebellious. On top of this there is no clear agreement on the way that the Holy Spirit is leading the family.

One day a beautiful 22-year-old woman comes to see John in the surgery. As he tries to help her, he realises that he is finding himself very attracted to her. He fights this feeling.

She has to return on a number of occasions. John realises that his feelings towards her are growing rather than diminishing. To complicate matters she is beginning to make it plain that she feels very attracted towards him.

The battle is now on. No-one knows what John is going through. How can he combat this situation that is rapidly getting out of control? Will he, like King David, end up in adultery?

John, fortunately, had the good sense to flee. Unable to

tell his wife of the pressure that he was under, he decided to go away to a distant place to stand in for another doctor as a locum. The family all assumed that he was just taking an opportunity to help in the Lord's work somewhere else for a while. The separation was enough to defuse the situation for John.

These pressures are all too common. So many of God's choicest servants have come to a tragic end along this line. We see some of those who have been greatly used by God and now seem to be a shadow of their former selves. They are withdrawn and no real blessing to anyone. We look and wonder and possibly criticise.

'There but for the grace of God go you or I.' The cycles of life hit out at all of us. For some women it may come every month in agonising depression over which they feel themselves to have little control. In some cases this is exacerbated by each monthly period itself being a reminder that they are still childless. Can they hold on to the promises of God that they will see 'the fruit of the travail of their soul and be satisfied'? Who is to criticise the person who, under these pressures, falls into depression or into sin?

Rather we need to reach out to God on such people's behalf. We can try to find ways to encourage them. We can try to build them up at a time when life seems to be pushing them down. We can express our belief in them when others are expressing their doubts.

'For it is not an enemy who reproaches me,
Then I could bear it;
Nor is it one who hates me who has exalted himself against me,
Then I could hide myself from him.
But it is you, a man my equal,
My companion and my familiar friend.
We who had sweet fellowship together,
Walking in the house of God in the throng' (Ps. 55:12-14).

What about the many who find no way to flee? Can we begin to look behind the facade to see that many are profoundly empty, insecure, lonely, and longing to know that they are still needed and wanted. Through David's darkest times there were some, admittedly few, who stuck by him. Their friendship and loyalty was probably the only barrier between his depression and frank despair. Without them he might have acted on the despair he felt in writing the following: 'My heart is in anguish within me, and terrors of death have fallen upon me. Fear and trembling come upon me; and horror has overwhelmed me. And I said, "Oh, that I had wings like a dove! I would fly away and be at rest. Behold, I would wander far away, I would lodge in the wilderness. I would hasten to my place of refuge from the stormy wind and tempest" ' (Ps. 55:4-6).

I know of no clearer indication that David was seriously contemplating suicide. He was desperate to find a way out of his situation. He was looking for anything that would give him some relief. What a blessing that he could find within himself and his friends enough confidence in God to end up by saying, 'Cast your burden upon the Lord, and He will sustain you; He will never allow the righteous to be shaken' (Ps. 55:22).

Endogenous Depression

A study of the psalms shows that David often felt himself betrayed and 'down'. Sometimes this was the result of his own folly and sin. Sometimes it was clearly through the active fault of others. In looking at the psalms though, one senses that at times he was just being put under pressure by Satan, the enemy of our souls. If Satan can find a chink in our armour through which to attack us, then you can be sure that he will. This is not so much a cause for fear, as for watchfulness.

I have already intimated earlier that I personally doubt if there is such a thing as true endogenous depression but it is quite clear that depression can hit at times for no obvious or discernable reason. My presumption at such times is that Satan has found a way to attack. I know that Satan wants to destroy us in any way that he can. Mainly through our own ignorance of the ways in which he attacks us, we find ourselves vulnerable.

An example of this in the life of David comes in Psalm 71. Here we have the heartcry of an old man who is feeling as if life, and the Lord, may be about to pass him by. 'Do not cast me off in the time of old age; Do not forsake me when my strength fails.'

How reminiscent of Elijah this is. In a time of great triumph and victory, he finds himself fearful that the Lord will let go of him (1 Kings 19:4). Somehow, our very victories can yield us vulnerable to attack. Maybe the Lord has allowed this so as to encourage our continued dependence on him. Maybe the pride of the moment opens us up subtly to attack from the enemy.

Whatever the cause that paves the way for depression to hit us, the cure is the same. 'Look to him and be radiant, and so your face need never be ashamed' (Ps. 34:5 AV). In his old age, David could still say with confidence, as yet another bout of depression and discouragement was attacking him, (possibly through the latest rebellion of one of his sons),

'By thee I have been sustained from my birth;
Thou art He who took me from my mother's womb;
My praise is continually of Thee' (Ps. 71:6).

Recently a Christian doctor friend of mine described to me two cases of people who had apparently proved resistant to all forms of help that he could offer. He had tried to minister to them in the power of the Holy Spirit. He had tried to pray against the obvious workings of the enemy within their lives with little success. Finally, in desperation, he had changed the antidepressant tablets that they had been on. To his amazement, both people had their mood clearly elevated within a couple of weeks, and seemed to be coping well with the pressures on their lives.

He was asking, as I also often have to ask, was the cure for their depression in the long run going to be through drugs? It is important to look at questions like this, and examples like this, so that we do not become 'so heavenly minded as to be no earthly use'.

To throw out all medication in depression (or any other 'illness') is probably counter-productive but to see the medication as the cure, rather than at best an aid in enabling the person to be healed is also counter-productive.

I doubt if antidepressants cure anyone. They may bring some people to a level where they can find the inner resources to deal with their depression. Psychotherapy, in bringing the roots of problems to the surface, may well do the same. However, the crucial element in healing is the power of the Holy Spirit.

Most people with depression, whether Christians or non-Christians, come to a point where spontaneously their depression lifts. In time it may recur in some; in others not necessarily so. We are never above the possibility that we may be hit by depression any more than we are above the possibility that any other illness may hit us. 'Therefore let him who thinks he stands take heed lest he fall' (1 Cor. 10:12).

We need neither complacency nor superiority as we face the attacks of depression that come our way. We need the word of God and the power of the Holy Spirit so that we can 'stand firm against the schemes of the devil' (Eph. 6:11).

9: Fears and Phobias

'For God has not given to us a spirit of fear, but of power and of love, and of a sound mind' (2 Tim. 1:7 AV).

I was driving along the three lane divided highway when the fear suddenly hit me out of the blue. I was in the fast lane, and so there were two other lanes of traffic on the inside between me and the edge of the road. I could see that the road was going up onto a large bridge that seemed to tower before me. The road had been built on a long causeway right across Tampa Bay, between Tampa and St. Petersburg, Florida. For about three miles the edge of the road was the ocean! It was rush hour and the highway was jam packed. Probably several hundred thousand cars crossed that causeway each day. But I knew as I went up the steep incline on the central bridge that I was about to lose my head for heights, and then lose control of the car.

My heart began to pound. I could feel my eyes constantly looking towards the edge of the road. I was hoping that I wouldn't hit too many other cars when I lost control. I was desperately praying - but with no success. By some super-human effort, or so it seemed, I was able to hold onto the steering wheel and navigate the car safely over the bridge. I could begin to breathe again normally. But what would it be like on the way back?

Felicity and I were visitors at the annual conference of the

Christian Medical Foundation International, based in Tampa, Florida. I had been invited over to speak. We thought we would use this opportunity to take the children over for a brief holiday, and to see my brother and his family.

While I was staying at the conference, Felicity and the children had been lent a lovely beach house in St Petersburg. They were sunbathing and swimming, while I was feasting on the abundant fare at the conference. The short distance between the hotel where the conference took place and the place where Felicity was staying could be covered in about twenty minutes, as long as one took this route straight across the bay.

I did not tell Felicity about this fear which had hit me, as I did not want to worry her. How often we are kept from freedom by fears of admitting our own weakness!

Driving back towards the same causeway was agony. I had come to the turning onto the causeway when I suddenly thought to myself, 'This fear is straight from "the pit". Satan is the author of fear, not the Lord. I am going to fight this thing.'

As I drove up towards the steep bridge I began singing and praising in tongues. I roundly rebuked the enemy. The fear continued to rise within me. I continued to praise and rejoice. I was over the hump of the bridge when I knew that I had broken the back of the fear! Satan was truly a defeated foe.

That night when addressing the conference, I found an unusual liberty in speaking about the goodness of the Lord, and of the necessity of acting in the power of the Holy Spirit.

Certainly 'God has not given us a spirit of fear'. Whenever fear hits us, or shows itself in others whom we are trying to help, we must ask ourselves where this fear comes from.

Fear, as with all other thoughts and emotions that we experience, can come from one of three sources. It can come from the Lord. It can come from ourselves. It can come from the enemy, Satan. Let's deal with the last of these fears first.

Fears from Satan

All fear that comes from Satan needs to be resisted. Fear is one of the enemy's prime ways of rendering us unavailable to God. Some of the most extrovert Christians, who will gladly speak to anyone about anything, find themselves speechless for fear of people when confronted with an opportunity to speak about their love of Jesus. Strong people, who would stand up to anyone for their political beliefs, become weak sheep when questioned about their faith!

This is not a natural phenomenon. Fear is one of the weapons that the enemy uses most efficiently against us. Often he seems to hit the target. Nearly always the fear finds a target in an area that we have thought about before, and regard as one of our potential weaknesses.

The fear of death is a clear example of how this works. Most of us are fearful of things that we do not know, have not experienced, and hence at best dimly understand. Death is one of those areas. One day a loved one unexpectedly dies. Perhaps it is a car crash, followed by a fire. Our minds begin to take hold of this event, and imagine ourselves in it. Because we do not know the power of our imagination, and so let it run away with our thoughts, we find that this scene is more and more frequently in our minds. Soon we find that we can hardly control our thoughts. They are always returning to this scene. Now any mention of our getting into a car can bring the fear on us. We are trapped in the fear. It began as a sensible, rational thought but it has become a true phobia. It is now irrational and totally unwanted. But we do not know how to get rid of it.

This imaginary scene is all too often played out in real life. A simple, but unpleasant situation leads us to yield a small part of our thinking to the devil. He takes the opportunity thus afforded (see the explanation of this concept in Ephesians 4:27 and earlier in this book), and begins to hold us captive.

James had had a very unhappy and unsettled childhood. He had been moved from foster home to foster home. No real security had been built into his life. At eighteen he was out on the street. As he had nowhere to go he began to wander around the country visiting various friends from the foster homes.

He had got as far as Leicester in his wanderings. He knocked at a friend's home, hoping for a place to stay for a few nights. As his friend answered the door, the friend had an epileptic fit. James was terrified. He had never seen epilepsy before, much less been aware that a friend of his suffered from it. From that moment onwards he began to fear that he would suffer from epilepsy. With increasing power this thought took hold of his life. Six months later James had his first epileptic fit!

Medically there is still so much that we do not begin to understand in these areas. The Bible has been showing us the way for centuries, but we are so unwilling to learn from it. 'For what I fear comes upon me, and what I dread befalls me. I am not at ease, nor am I quiet, And I am not at rest, but turmoil comes' (Job 3:25-26).

Fear seems to prepare the ground for the very thing we fear to come and dominate our lives. Most of these fears are clearly lies, sent to us from the father of lies. But if we let them gain control of the way that we think then they may begin to be enacted before us.

Often in counselling people with fears, we find a clear beginning to the fear. It may have been precipitated by an incident such as being locked in a cupboard by a parent as a punishment in childhood. It may be a fear that hits one suddenly and inexplicably as in my own experience with the sudden fear of driving over the very tall bridge. It may be a fear that grips one while watching a horror film, or going into a seance or some other occult experience. Nowadays fear frequently attacks drug abusers when they have a bad trip.

Having found the source, we need to cut the person free by binding the power of the evil spirits that have used that incident to bring the person into bondage. Jesus has given us 'authority to tread upon serpents and scorpions, and over all the power of the enemy, and nothing shall injure you. Nevertheless do not rejoice in this, that the spirits are subject to you, but rejoice that your names are recorded in heaven' (Lk. 10:19-20).

We need to guard our minds, and teach others how to guard their minds. Fear, once it gets its tentacles attached to us, does not like to let go. The very fear tends towards producing the thing that is feared.

I have wondered if, at a spiritual level, this is one way that illnesses of both the body and the soul may be passed from one generation to another. Familial spirits, wanting to continue the process of destruction that they have started in one generation, may try to put pressure on us to fear that we will end up with the same problem or illness that our parents had. As we dwell on the fear, the spiritual forces of wickedness may be able to latch onto our body or mind in such a way as to begin to cause that illness to work in us.

Obviously, at a physical level there may be genetic changes that can be studied under the microscope. There may be a biochemical defect which is passed on from one generation to another. But we know that the realm of the physical is not the final arbiter of reality. Behind it, and hidden from the realm of the natural mind, is this realm of the spirit. It may well be that what we see played out in the natural realm has its specific counterpart in the realm of the spirit.

If we take the Scriptures seriously, we see why we need to learn to 'bring every thought captive to Christ'. We want to be those who rest secure, protected by the wonderful armour that the Lord has given to us.

Fears from Ourself

Not all fear has its origin in Satan. Much even of what he burdens us with really has its inception in what we do and see. However, not all of this is necessarily harmful.

A child that puts its hand into a lovely-looking fire will learn to fear the fire. And so it should. A natural fear of that which can harm us is a very useful protection against some of the more dangerous things that we might otherwise get involved with. Many Christians have a healthy fear of things that may lead them into sin, and rightly so. This does not mean that fear dominates our lives. It means that we have enough respect for the power of sin and the power of the devil, not to go flirting with areas where we are likely to be vulnerable.

For example, recently converted alcoholics are unlikely to find that their ministry is to work in pubs to help others find Christ. They rightly fear the pull of that environment on them. We learn to 'save others, snatching them out of the fire; and on some have mercy with fear, hating even the garment polluted by the flesh' (Jude 23). How tragic it is when a fine Christian man, trying to help those who have been pushed into prostitution, finds himself becoming the latest conquest of the prostitute! None of us should consider ourselves as immune from attack in any given area.

However, other fears that may equally easily have their source in ourselves are often most unhelpful. Many of us are dogged by fear of what others think about us. We may long to be free to shape others, but find instead that we are much more likely to be shaped by them. Even with a clear call of God upon our lives, we have to push through this fear of people to a position where we will allow ourselves to choose only to fear God.

Moses found himself in just this situation. He had been signalled out by God from his infancy. He had been trained in the best private schools of his day. No doubt he won first prize in his public speaking examinations. But when it came to the possibility of having to face others with what God wanted to say to them, his reply to God was, 'Who am I that I should go to Pharoah, and that I should bring the sons of Israel out of Egypt?'

Even God's assurance that He would go with him was not enough. 'What if they will not believe me, or listen to what I say? For they may say, "The Lord has not appeared to you." '

So the Lord explains to Moses that He will be confirming Moses' word with powerful signs and wonders. Still Moses finds that he is too fearful to proceed and tries to evade the call of God on his life. 'Please, Lord, I have never been eloquent, neither recently nor in time past, nor since Thou hast spoken to Thy servant; for I am slow of speech and slow of tongue' (Ex. 4:10).

Quite frankly, I don't believe Moses. He was a skilled leader. He was brave enough to attack and kill an Egyptian soldier who was hurting one of his fellow countrymen. But he was still scared to tell people what God was putting on his heart. Finally in desperation he says to God, 'Please, Lord, now send the message by whomever You will' (Ex. 4:13). In other words, 'Please use anybody but me!'

The truth is that we are little different from Moses. We too have been promised that 'signs and wonders' would follow our proclamation of the good news that we have to share with others (Mk. 16:17-20). We too have the promise that 'He will never leave us or forsake us' (Heb. 13:5). We too have His assurance that His word will be in our mouths when we need it (Mt. 10:19). So we too sometimes need the anger of the Lord to burn against us as it did against Moses (Ex. 4:14), so that we will start to speak when he asks us to speak.

It was an incident rather like the above sequence that finally brought me out of hiding and into an attitude where I was prepared to take whatever opportunities that the Lord gave to me through my professional work as a doctor.

It was the winter of 1976. I was doing my first hospital job, working as a house-physician. We were in the middle of a flu epidemic, and were working all day and often most of the night also.

Mr Jones was admitted in poor condition, with pneumonia having developed from the flu. One day, while I was examining him, he had a cardiac arrest. We immediately resuscitated him, and admitted him to the intensive care unit. Slowly over the next weeks he was nursed back to health.

On his last day in the ward he called me over. He presented me with a small package. 'I know that I cannot give you anything, so I have brought you a small present for your wife. You have saved my life, and I so appreciate all the love and attention that you have given to me.'

As I thought about what he said, God began to speak to me. 'Mr Jones has only seen you. He has not seen the one who made you like you are. "I am the Lord, my glory I will share with no other" ' (Is. 42:8).

I realised that although I was generally liked by staff and

patients alike, and although they gave me all the credit for being a 'decent sort of fellow', if I did not speak about Jesus, they would have no way of knowing that it was Jesus who was at work in me to make me the way I was. For 'how shall they hear without a preacher?' (Rom. 10:14).

Now I saw that it is not enough for us to say that we will show others the Lord Jesus by the quality of our lives. We must also speak about Him. For 'faith comes by hearing, and hearing by the word of Christ' (Rom. 10:17).

We are all called to be witnesses to the Lord Jesus Christ. The baptism in the Holy Spirit is first and foremost intended to empower us to be a bold testimony to the power of God in our lives. We see in the disciples that their fear of other people was dealt a death blow by the baptism in the Holy Spirit. This did not, however, stop them from praying again and again that the Lord would give them still more boldness!

Very few, it seems, naturally find it easy to talk about the Lord Jesus. Most will have to learn to overcome the fears that prevent us from telling others about Jesus. For the Christian professional, there is going to be the added fear of what colleagues or our professional bodies may say about us using our position to share Christ. It seems to me that we can only, like the apostles, state that 'we cannot stop speaking what we have seen and heard' (Acts 3:20).

A friend of mine was warned some time ago that he would lose his job as a probation officer if he continued to speak about the Lord Jesus with the young people he was dealing with. He agreed that he would not bring the subject up, but clearly stated that if he was asked about his own faith, or about 'religion', he would have to be honest about his own position. The authorities agreed to this. He began asking the Lord that the young people who were being assigned to him would bring up this area. He found that he was having as many, or more opportunities, under this new restriction than he had had before!

Not all will be given the same permission. Very recently, at a Caring Professions Concern conference, a young physiotherapist told us how she was facing a disciplinary committee for sharing her faith while working with patients. A senior consultant gynaecologist, whom I know well, was recently made to answer to a panel of senior consultants and administrators for the way that she handled abortion requests that came her way.

Some, in time, will probably have to pay the price of losing their jobs as they learn to be bold and stand up for Jesus. We must ask the Lord to work in us so that we will willingly stand with them. Jesus told his disciples that they would find themselves standing before 'kings and governors' (Mt. 10:18). That is going to be true for some today as they take a strong stand for the present rule of Christ in human affairs.

How do we deal with these anxieties that arise out of ourselves, and render us liable to fear? I want people to know that God is on their side, He is going to see them through to a position of victory.

'What then shall we say to these things? If God is for us, who is against us? He who did not spare His own Son, but delivered Him up for us all, how will He not also with Him freely give us all things?' (Rom. 8:31,32).

'For I am confident of this very thing, that He who began good work in you will perfect it until the day of Christ Jesus' (Phil. 1:6).

How contrary so much of this apparently is to our personal experience! And how much more important it is that we hold on to the living and abiding word of God rather than to our experience! It is we who need to change, not the word of God. We are being transformed into His image; His word is not being transformed into our image.

As the word of God begins to get right deep down inside us, we find that it meets with a response from the Holy Spirit within. 'Deep calls to deep at the sound of Thy waterfalls' (Ps. 42:7). And so we find from deep within us a response of our spirit to the presence of the Spirit of God as the living water from God's presence flows into our inner beings to transform us.

The word of God, spoken out, is very powerful. It is no accident that we often see in the Old Testament that the people had the law read out aloud to them. As we have seen earlier, 'But the righteousness based on faith *speaks* thus'. We need to learn the power that is available when we openly confess the word of God to be true for us and for others.

As we counsel others they need to hear much from our lips of the word of God. They will almost certainly have had much good advice from other people. Now give to them the word of God.

This feeding ourselves from the word of God is totally complementary to the parallel feeding that goes on direct from the Spirit of God to our spirit. Again we have an active part in this feeding process, even though it is the Spirit of God who feeds us! It seems that God does not want any of us to get lazy.

'But you, beloved, building yourselves up on your most holy faith; praying in the Holy Spirit' (Jude 20). Most people who have tried praying in tongues for any extended periods of time have testified both to the difficulty and blessing that follows. There is no doubt in my own mind that, as we learn to make 'tongues' a backdrop to all that we do, we will find the presence of Christ coming more and more powerfully into every part of our daily walk.

Praying in tongues seems to renew and refresh us at every level. How we underestimate the preciousness of each gift that God gives to us! If we look back at the context of the Isaiah 28 passage quoted in 1 Corinthians 14 as applying to the gift of tongues, we find that in tongues there 'is rest, give rest to the weary. Here is repose' (Is. 28:12).

I think that it was David Wilkerson who related the truth of this in one of his books. In the early days when he began to travel around a lot, speaking about some of the things that the Lord was doing, he was getting very tired from not sleeping on the long coach trips. The Lord told him to use the time while travelling to pray in tongues. He was still not sleeping any more than usual on the trips. But he was arriving refreshed in body and spirit!

It has been a great joy to see many who have been severely weakened in their minds and spirits brought back into a position of strength as they used this gift. 'Do not neglect the spiritual gift within you, which was bestowed upon you through prophetic utterance with the laying on of hands' (1 Tim. 5:14).

Fear from God

We now need to look briefly at a third source from which fear can come. It is good to remember that not all fear is either evil or negative.

'And everyone kept feeling a sense of awe; and many wonders and signs were taking place through the apostles' (Acts 5:11-12).

'The fear of the Lord is the beginning of knowledge; Fools despise wisdom and instruction' (Prov. 1:7).

'So David was afraid of the Lord that day' (2 Sam. 6:9) – the story of how the Lord struck down Uzzah for touching the ark of the convenant).

'And great fear came upon the whole church, and upon all who heard of these things. And at the hands of the

Apostles many signs and wonders were taking place among the people (Acts 5:11-12).

We have a much appreciated familiarity with the Lord. We love Him and we often tell Him so. But do we fear Him? Do we understand His terrible majesty and power? There is certainly much to learn here for those of us who have been so blessed in the present move of the Holy Spirit. God calls this fear the actual starting place in our coming into a knowledge of Him.

We see this working out in the relationship that our children have to us. Of course we want them to love us. We long to move in an easy familiarity with them that leads to openness and loving acceptance of each other. However, there is also the need for respect and even awe. Children are to obey their parents. Sometimes it is the fear of the rod that leads to the willing obedience!

In the early portions of the book of Acts we see the people of Jerusalem thrilled and terrified by this Jesus whom they had just crucified. The healing of the lame man brought much rejoicing, but the slaying of Ananias and Sapphira scared everyone equally as much.

As we see more and more of the power of God released among us, I believe that this fear, along with a deepening love and commitment, will be a hallmark of the living presence of Christ among us.

10: Sexuality

'Let marriage be held in honour among all, and let the marriage bed be undefiled; for fornicators and adulterers God will judge' (Heb. 13:4).

He was a young leader within his church. He was held in high regard by all who knew him both within the church and within his professional life. When he came to speak to me at the end of the meeting, I had no idea what was on his mind.

'Tony, I have got to have a word with you privately.'

Then out it all came. He was engaged to a lovely girl. But they both knew that their walk with the Lord was being ruined because they were sleeping together. How could he break out of this sinful habit that they had fallen into? Possibly most revealing, and to me most tragic, was his remark, 'It was really difficult the first time that I slept with a girl; the Lord was powerfully working on my conscience to prevent me. But it has been so easy since then!'

On another occasion, a young woman came to see me. With tears in her eyes she told me that she and her husband were having some difficulty in their sexual relationship, and it seemed to be affecting every other part of their relationship with each other and with the Lord. She was sure that it had begun because on a couple of occasions they had slept together before they were married. They had come to the Lord for forgiveness, but they still sensed that the immorality had some hold on their lives. She felt that her confession to me as a church leader would help her to know that this past sin was genuinely dealt with (Jn. 20:23).

A young man came to see me at home. He knew that the Bible did not allow homosexual behaviour, but he could not see why he had to change when this was the way that the Lord had made him! As we talked I could see him trying to grapple with an area where the Holy Spirit was putting His finger on him. This young man's cultural environment told him that his way of life was just a normal variant. The Holy Spirit was clearly telling him otherwise.

Similar heresies crept into the New Testament churches within years of them being established. They have continued to crop up among the Lord's people ever since. Solomon was absolutely right when he said:
'That which has been is that which will be,
And that which has been done is that which will be done.
So there is nothing new under the sun.
Is there anything of which one might say,
'See this, it is new'?
Already it has existed for ages
Which were before us' (Eccles. 1:9,10).

I heard Ken Humphreys, the pastor of the Praise Community Churches, talking about sexuality on one occasion. He pointed out that apart from the desire for survival, there did not seem to be any stronger instinctive drive than sex. The first thing that our common parents, Adam and Eve, realised when they had eaten the forbidden fruit was that they were naked. Presumably before this they were attracted to each other, for Adam was thrilled when he saw the wife God had prepared for him. But now his sexuality became tainted. It had a 'dirty' aspect to it. It became something that they had to hide. And people have been hiding ever since.

It must be clearly stated that sex, like all else that God has created, is beautiful. It is marred by what we, with Satan's help, have done to it. We have taken of the glory of God's creation, perverted it, elevated it to the place of a 'god', and then found that when we moved outside of God's laws, we always reap the results of our sin.

The very oneness that belongs to a husband and wife as they 'know' each other, to use the rather quaint language of the Bible, becomes instead a barrier to real loving commitment and trust when used before marriage. Instead of drawing couples closer together, it sows the seeds of mistrust. After all, if they do not respect each other enough to wait until the time God has given, how will they know for sure that they respect each other enough to be loyal after they have married? So many couples go into their marriages with the wonder and joy of exploring their sexuality already behind them. Many find that this reaps its own reward of difficulty in finding the depth of relationship that they had hoped for.

This is not to minimise the place of repentance and forgiveness. It is rather a recognition that what has been done cannot be undone. Our sins are forgiven, but the consequences often remain. David was forgiven for the incident with Bathsheba, but Uriah was still dead, and the baby conceived in adultery still died. Would it be stretching the point too far to say that in Solomon, the wisest man who ever lived, there continued this fatal flaw of promiscuity that finally became his undoing? See 1 Kings 11:4 : 'For it came about when Solomon was old, his wives turned his heart away after other gods; and his heart was not wholly devoted to the Lord his God, as the heart of David his father had been'.

The Bible is totally real in the way that it portrays human

sexuality. Marriage is held up as honourable and beautiful. It is a picture of the relationship that Christ will have with us, His bride (Eph. 5:22-33). What God has in mind as our union with Him after the marriage supper of the Lamb can only be beauty beyond beauties. They very picture that He paints for us of healthy sexuality in the Song of Songs shows us that God desires the best for us in the beauty of the relationships that He has made us for.

However, the ugliness of relationships when they go wrong is also plainly there for all to see. Amnon was one of King David's sons. He had a beautiful half-sister whose name was Tamar. Amnon could not control his passionate desire for her. One day, he pretended to be ill and asked Tamar to come and nurse him. When all the other people had left the room he forced his attentions on her, raping her. This resulted in a dramatic change in his attitude to her. 'Then Amnon hated her with a very great hatred; for the hatred with which he hated her was greater than the love with which he had loved her. And Amnon said to her, "Get up, go away" ' (2 Sam. 13:15).

Incest here was rapidly producing its bitter fruit, which ended up with murder. Suspicion breeds like mosquitoes in a swamp when people begin to allow their sexuality to come out from under the restraints that God has put on it.

Adultery

Frequently in the surgery I have a wife or husband come in and say that they will never be able to trust their partner again. A brief adulterous encounter leaves a lasting legacy, even after forgiveness has been given. Trust needs the healing work of the Spirit to come to fruition. Time does not heal; rather with time, God does the healing. Some people never come back into a relationship of full love and reconciliation.

Paul, in referring to these areas, warned us: 'Every other sin that a man commits is outside the body, but the immoral man sins against his own body' (1 Cor. 6:18). Never is this more clearly seen than when a husband or wife betrays the trust of their partner, and the 'one flesh' finds itself 'put asunder'. There are more ways than divorce of dividing 'what God has put together'.

'Can a man take fire in his bosom,
And his clothes not be burned?
Or can a man walk on hot coals,
And his feet not be scorched?
So is the one who goes in to his neighbour's wife:
Whoever touches her will not go unpunished.
Men do not despise a thief if he steals
To satisfy himself when he is hungry;
But when he is found, he must repay sevenfold;
He must give all the substance of his house.
The one who commits adultery with a woman is lacking in
    sense;
He who would destroy himself does it.
Wounds and disgrace he will find,
And his reproach will not be blotted out.
For jealousy enrages a man,
And he will not spare in the day of vengeance.
He will not accept any ransom,
Nor will he be content though you give many gifts'
    (Prov. 6:27-35).

Much counselling turns out to be unabashed sentiment-ality, rather than a true biblical sharing of the word of the Lord. We may try to calm troubled waters, but this will not happen except at the voice of the Lord. Unless we teach clearly what the word of God says, we will find our churches filled with the bitter fruits of this sin.

If there are two main areas in which Christian leaders are

most likely to fail, they are sex and money. So many of those who have done great things in the power of God have found themselves subsequently broken on the rocks of immorality. Great leaders, whom we have so badly needed to help lead the Church on into maturity, have fallen, sometimes not to return to the fight, because of the depth of wounds that they have received in this area.

The first counsel to any who come to us with this as a potential problem area is to 'flee youthful lusts' (2 Tim. 2:22). Many years ago my wife and I made a vow to each other - and we take any vow as totally binding in the sight of God. We said that if we began to find some person of the opposite sex particularly attractive, we would immediately tell our partner. This has had the effect of defusing any potentially dangerous situation that may have developed.

What can we counsel though when the situation has already gone past the 'potential' into the 'actual'? First it is worth being aware that there are probably four people who need help. The person coming to you, the marriage partner, the person with whom they have committed adultery, and that person's marriage partner. Both marriages probably had something amiss to begin with for this situation to have developed. Both will need great openness, loving forgiveness, and a true measure of repentance, if the situation is to be resolved. It is unrealistic to expect that life can carry straight on as normal. If any of the people involved are engaged in leadership within the body of Christ, then it is vital that they find a way quietly and unobtrusively to lay down these responsibilities so as to put their own marriage back together.

A good marriage is the *sine qua non* for any form of Christian leadership. When we begin to play down the importance of the instructions that Paul gave to us on this subject, we begin to destroy all effective discipline within the body of Christ. For 'if a man does not know how to manage his own household, how will he take care of the church of God?' (1 Tim. 3:5).

Private sin needs to be dealt with privately. But if the sin is common knowledge, then it will need to be dealt with publicly. A church that sweeps sin under the carpet, be it private or public, is a church that will have its 'candlestick' removed by the living Christ (Rev. 2:5).

Some time ago, the leaders of the church of which I was then a part had an evening together to wait on the Lord. As we spent this time together, the Lord spoke to us clearly from Revelation 2. We had just had a number of women come to the Lord. All were heavily involved in immorality and adultery, and were having difficulty dealing with this area of their past lives. The Lord made it plain to us that we could not expect to turn a blind eye to this needy area in their lives just because they were all such young Christians. The Lord told us that he would remove his presence from us if we did not deal with this sin among us.

We were not sure how best to deal with this. So we continued to pray, and to ask the Holy Spirit to show us how He wanted it dealt with. The Lord showed us that we were to pray for such a manifestation of the holiness of God that the women would either come to true repentance and cleansing, or else would leave the church, unable to cope with the presence of God.

That is just what happened. About a week later one of them rang me up.

'Tony,' she said, 'You know that I love the Lord. But I am going to have to stop coming to the meetings. I am not ready to give up . . . . and I can't keep coming and being a hypocrite.'

She then went on to name two others whom she had brought to the Lord and who had been coming to church with her. She told me that they were going to stop coming as well, for the same reasons.

I pleaded with her to deal with the sin, but knew that it was better to lose her than lose the presence of God.

Promiscuity

It is generally conceded that fads which originate in either England or the United States take about two years successfully to cross the Atlantic. This period of time is probably becoming shorter and shorter with the improvements in telecommunication that we have nowadays.

I would say that a similar time-lag seems to describe how long it takes the values of the world to become normal within the church! From the earliest part of the book of Exodus it is clear that it is far easier to get the children of Israel out of Egypt, than it is to get 'Egypt' out of the children of Israel!

With the welcome influx of new converts that many churches are seeing today, there comes an even greater responsibility to build into these people the principles of the word of God. Old ways spread rapidly. As Haggai made plain, uncleanness is highly contagious, holiness is not! (Hag. 2:13).

As young people come to us looking for help in these areas, how can we advise them? Does the Bible give us clear guidelines? The answer is an unequivocal 'Yes'. Holiness of life and thought is the biblical standard. Marriage is to be lifted up as honourable. Sexual passions are to be kept under control.

'Do not arouse or awaken love, until it please' (Song 2:7) seems to be a sensible approach. We all know how easily our passions are aroused. So we need to exercise caution in what we do if we don't want our passions to overwhelm us.

From the way many Christians live, you would think that the biblical approach is for us to live as near to the world as we can. We don't do anything 'sinful', but we get as close to sin as we can. This is not only living dangerously, but foolishly. We may easily find that the uncleanness manages to catch us, rather than that we manage to preserve and extend the 'holiness without which no man shall see the Lord' (Heb. 12:14).

Perversions

As modern men and women let go of what little restraint our culture puts on them, we find people becoming involved with all sorts of perversions. You will not counsel people for long now without hearing confessions about incest, pornography, sodomy, bestiality, bondage, and every other type of perversion. Perversions leave deep scars in people's lives, both in those who deliberately propagate them, and in the victims of these perverted ways. Great love and compassion is needed in encouraging people to open up to you so that you can help them to come to Jesus for healing and deliverance.

John and Paula Sandford, in their fascinating book, *The Transformation of the Inner Man*, describe how there are demonic principalities that govern the thought patterns of whole sub-cultures in our society. They show how, in areas such as homosexuality, the whole pattern of thinking is clearly anti-God in its most fundamental values.

Within some of our big towns and cities the homosexual community is so powerful that they are recognised as a distinct minority grouping of their own. In one inner London borough, the council proudly tell us that homosexuals are a clear minority grouping with their own 'rights'. Another council may by now have the dubious distinction of being the first London borough to have a male 'mayoress'. The new mayor plans to install his male partner as any other mayor would his wife.

This blatantly perverted sexuality is a reenactment of the depravity that was the norm in the latter part of Rome's fall from power. It is the same departure from the ways of God that signalled the end for Sodom and Gomorrah. Parts of many ancient empires, when coming into their decline, were predominantly homosexual in their outlook.

As long as we describe homosexuality as a sickness, we will look in vain for a form of healing. Medicine has little to offer to bring a cure. Because of this, most people now take the next obvious step, and say that homosexuality is just a variant of the normal, so it does not need healing. We already see the elements of this type of thinking widely accepted in other areas. Frequently in sociology textbooks one can see the idea that society is the culprit, and the poor criminals cannot be blamed for falling into crime. Presumably 'society' is everyone except the authors and their friends!

When we reject the truth about God, that is 'evident within us', then it is only a short time before we become 'fools' by 'exchanging the truth of God for a lie, and worship and serve the creature rather than the Creator . . . For this reason God gave them over to degrading passions; for their women exchanged the natural function for that which is unnatural, and in the same way also the men abandoned the natural function of the woman and burned in their desire toward one another, men with men committing indecent acts and receiving in their own persons the due penalty of their error' (Rom. 1:24-27).

Most Christians are unaware of the extent of the promiscuity which is the norm among those who are into deviant practices. A typical heterosexual who comes into a venereal diseases clinic will have three to four partners who need to be traced to try to prevent the spread of disease. With most homosexuals there could be ten to a hundred recent contacts to be traced, though homosexuals have recently begun to establish more 'stable' one-to-one relationships because of the fear of catching AIDS if sexually involved with many partners.

God loves people, but he still hates sin, whatever name we give it. A short time ago one of the young men in the fellowship at home came to chat to me. He had been plagued by feeling himself to be homosexual. As we talked this over he began to see that the way he conceived of himself would have a powerful effect on the sort of person that he would become. By focusing on an area of apparent weakness, he was playing right into Satan's hands. 'But each one is tempted when he is carried away and enticed by his own lust. Then when lust has conceived, it gives birth to sin; and when sin is accomplished, it brings forth death' (Js. 1:14:15).

The sin is not the initial lustful thought. It comes out of dwelling on that thought until it is 'conceived' and the actual sin ensues. In counselling those who have found themselves drawn into these areas, it is important to try to understand why they have wanted to behave in this way. Sometimes it is because of insecurities that have begun showing through because of very poor relationships with their own parents. Sometimes it is because they were introduced to homosexuality at an early age by a sibling, family member, or family friend who has taken advantage of their innocence. Sometimes it is the end result of deliberate exploration into immorality which has led to needing more and more deviation to produce the same 'excitement' that they initially experienced.

The Holy Spirit is well able both to pinpoint the source

of the deviation and give the release that is needed from the hold of these sins. Unless we see these areas as sin we are unlikely to come to Christ to find His power to be set free. Having seen these areas as sin, though, we need all the love and compassion that would be afforded to anyone else trapped in sin, and trying to find their way out. 'Brethren, even if a man is caught in any trespass, you who are spiritual, restore such a one in a spirit of gentleness' (Gal. 6:1).

Many young homosexuals already have a very low opinion of thesmselves. The last thing that they need is further condemnation and criticism. They may have come to you just because they know that they need help. 'Bear one another's burdens, and thus fulfil the law of Christ' (Gal. 6:2). We can demonstrate the Lord's love to people without condoning the sin that traps them.

Masturbation

This is probably a good place to say a word about masturbation. Very frequently young men (and older ones too) have come to me to ask about this area that they perceive as a big problem in their lives. While it is true that the Bible seems to say nothing specific regarding masturbation itself, it clearly does say a lot about our thought life and controlling our passions. While it may be better for a man to relieve sexual tension by masturbation than risking immorality, it is still entering into a risky area. I, for one, would hesitate to say that masturbation, *per se*, is wrong. What is wrong is the grip that it holds on so many, and the fantasies that are the usual accompaniment.

Some Christian leaders have suggested that for a man away from his wife, masturbation may be a legitimate way of releasing some of the tension that tends to build up. Similarly, for an unmarried man, some would say that masturbation will help to make sure that they do not enter into immorality. I am not so sure. What is clear is that masturbation does have a strong tendency to dominate any person who practises it. As God has built into men a natural way of releasing the build up of sexual tension in 'wet dreams', we are probably safest in not practising masturbation at all.

Female masturbation, while not as common as in men, is still a considerable problem to some. Walter Trobish, in his book, *My Beautiful Feeling*, tries to come to grips with some the issues that we have looked at above. While his conclusions are perhaps not as dogmatic as mine, they form a very helpful starting place in discussing this area with anyone, male or female, who comes to you for help.

Pornography

Pornography is another area where people can so easily be caught unawares. Some time ago there was an excellent article in one of the leading Christian magazines by a man who had begun by peeping at dirty pictures, and had ended up being involved in perverted sex with children. This led to a police charge against him. Little sins so easily become bigger. We need to deal with sins as soon as they show themselves. Unfortunately our shame and our pride often prevent us admitting that we are having a problem in an area like pornography.

It is so vital that those who come to us for counsel with this sort of problem find us accepting of them, uncondemning, *and yet uncompromising*. People do not need to be hit over the head, but neither are they asking to be let off. They come to us wanting to be set free. People are unlikely to be helped by us if we appear shocked by everything that they tell us. Neither do they find release through our sympathy. Security comes as they know that we will help them find the power of Christ to free them from the bondage they are in.

In all of these areas we want to help point people to healthy alternatives to the sin that may attract them. Much can be done to encourage groups of single Christians to spend time together in such a way that they will not put pressure on each other to be always in pairs. We can point people to more sensible life-styles, such as not spending a lot of time alone with their boy or girlfriends in a situation where it is unlikely that anyone else will be around. We can help people see that there is so much that is good and helpful that we can read, that we do not have to fill our minds with television, immorality and various forms of pornography. We can seek to encourage an attitude where chastity is not sniggered at, but admired. We can teach a self-restraint and respect for each other that so highly esteems those of the opposite sex, that we will respect their purity.

Above all we can point people towards a love for Christ that is so all-consuming that we will seriously consider counting all things 'as loss for the sake of Christ' (Phil. 3:7). It is not that sex is not entirely legitimate - rather that we want to make sure that our priorities are right.

Frequently for those who are happily married and actively involved in the work of the Kingdom there will be times, perhaps extended times, when they will need to hold the pleasure of sex in abeyance because of the need to be available to minister. Even here the Bible, ever practical, tells us not to 'deprive one another, except by agreement for a time that you may devote yourselves to prayer, and come together again lest Satan tempt you because of your lack of self-control' (1 Cor. 7:5).

Our sexuality is a wonderful expression of God's delight in His creation. When we express our sexuality within the framework of God's purity, we find our lives wonderfully enriched and blessed.

11: Epilepsy and Psychotic Illness

'And the news about Him went out into all Syria; and they brought to Him all who were ill, taken with various diseases and pains, demoniacs, epileptics, paralytics: and He healed them' (Mt. 4:24).

Epilepsy

We were in a small meeting place just opposite the cathedral in Birmingham. I had been asked to speak at the meeting by my friend, Nick Cuthbert. As he was about to introduce me, we heard a commotion outside the hall. I popped out to see what was happening, and found a young man having an epileptic fit in the hallway.

Nick joined me outside. I'm not sure who was leading the meeting from then on. We asked the young man how he had happened to come into the building. He told us that he had just been passing the building when he had felt a sudden, very strong urge to come inside and find out what was going on. He had that day come out of mental hospital where they had been treating him because he was hearing voices. He was in the process of coming into the hall where the meeting was going on when he had this fit. No, he didn't normally suffer from fits as far as he was aware.

We were very inexperienced in this sort of thing. I was

still in medical school. Fortunately I was too junior to be able to make any real medical diagnosis of what was going on. So presuming that the Lord had allowed this to happen, we began to tell Peter that the Lord Jesus could set him free both from the voices and the fits. He was most keen for us to pray.

As we began to pray, Peter had another fit! We commanded this 'thing' to let go of him. As he calmed down, we told him more of what it meant to be a follower of the Lord Jesus. We continued to pray, and in about half an hour he was set completely free.

This was quite an introduction to these things for a young medical student and his pastor friend! To be honest, we had seen something of demonic powers prior to this, but always when there were others around who were experienced. All of a sudden we were being thrown into the deep end ourselves. Experience is often the best school of Christian counselling.

In the first part of this book we looked quite fully at the whole question of what framework, or worldview, we begin with in looking at a problem. Nowhere in medicine and psychiatry does this seem to me to be more relevant than when we look at epilepsy. The word translated as epileptic in our New Testaments is actually, literally, 'Moon-stricken' (see marginal reading of Mt. 4:24).

To say that we can show on an electro-encephalogram (EEG) abnormal waves over certain areas of the brain is actually begging the question. What we want to know is what are those abnormal brain waves doing there? How do they trigger the epileptic attack? The abnormal waves may be there because an accident has scarred a small portion of the brain. In that case, medically, we would call this 'post-traumatic epilepsy'. Such epilepsy is quite common following severe head injuries. A tumour may be growing in part of the brain, and as it pushes on the surrounding tissues, it could cause problems. We may have no idea at all why the EEG shows a focus at a specific location. A person may even suffer from epilepsy without the neurologists being able to demonstrate any specific abnormality on the EEG.

Where does the realm of the Spirit impinge on this? How do we explain at a physical or biochemical level the mechanism whereby an epileptic, who is well controlled on such a drug as Phenytoin, can find himself in a meeting where he is set free when prayed for in the name of Jesus? Did the drug suppress a demonic manifestation?

In the final analysis, any action that we see, any change in a person's physical or mental state, may have a physical cause whereby it took place. Behind this, though, is the whole realm of the spirit. It is like watching a Punch and Judy show, and becoming so engrossed in the action of the puppets that one forgets that there is a person who is manipulating the puppets behind the scenes. We see the physical, but behind that is the whole unseen realm of the spiritual.

We tend to think of the 'real' world as that which we can see, but the Bible describes the 'real' world as the realm of the spirit. 'While we look not at the things which are seen, but at the things which are not seen, for the things which are seen are temporal, but the things which are not seen are eternal' (2 Cor. 4:18).

Elisha's servant was trapped in the world that he could see, and so feared for his own life and the life of his master in the story in 2 Kings 6. When his eyes were opened - if you like, when his world view was altered - he saw the army of God's angels around the enemy and realised that he and Elisha were in fact quite safe.

A friend of mine, who is also a general practitioner, rang

129

me up after seeing an article I wrote on epilepsy suggesting that it is sometimes caused by demonic powers. In his church they have quite a number of epileptics who come to their meetings. There is a residential care centre nearby for those who are severely affected by epilepsy. This friend told me that they used to find that the epilepsy would often show itself in the meeting at a time which seemed to make for maximum disruption.

They began praying about this and felt that they should take active control over the epilepsy in the name of Jesus. They have since found that the frequency of attacks has been drastically cut down. Interestingly, they have also found that if an attack does come, it lasts only a very short while.

To imply from these stories that all epilepsy is caused by demons (except possibly in the ultimate sense that all illness finds its root in Satan's work), is unnecessarily simplistic. However, to turn one's mind away from the reality that much epilepsy, and other diseases, may have a clear demonic cause, is not only hiding our heads in the sand, but also denying freedom to many who would find it if someone would pray for them.

We need the gift of discernment. We also need a new boldness to go along with it. Jesus 'went about doing good, and healing all who were oppressed by the devil; for God was with Him' (Acts 10:38). As we begin to encounter people who suffer from the same problems now that Jesus dealt with in His days on earth, we will find that the cure for them is also the same.

There is a tendency in some circles to imply that, as Jesus lived two thousand years ago, he was trapped in the limited knowledge of the time. There is obviously some truth to this, as he would have thought and tended to react in the same way as people around him. However, to limit

Jesus like this is to disregard the effect that being in constant touch with His Father had on Him. In fact, His very nonscientific framework may have made it easier for Him to believe His Father when He told Him that a problem was based in the spirit realm. Certainly, it does seem that the more that we allow the word of God to get inside us, the more we realise that we do 'not wrestle against flesh and blood, but against the rulers, against the powers, against the world forces of this darkness, against the spiritual forces of wickedness in the heavenly places' (Eph. 6:12).

Although it is often helpful to know how a person's epilepsy started, and beyond that to begin to understand the 'whys and wherefores', it is by no means essential. I remember a young auxiliary nurse whose epilepsy began at a party. Whether she had been involved in anything wrong herself I honestly do not know. But the surrounding circumstances seemed to play some part in opening her up to the attack of epilepsy.

I mentioned in the chapter on fear, the situation of the young man who witnessed an epileptic attack in a friend, and found himself paralysed by the fear that this would attack him next. Another example of this clear association between an event and epilepsy is seen in the epilepsy that afflicts some people from demon-worshipping cultures.

Ali is a young man who came from an Indian Sikh background. He was actively involved in the worship of the Guru Nanock, and had been to various shrines while living in India. The priests of these heathen deities had prayed over him on a number of occasions.

Ali was having two distinct types of 'epileptic' attacks. He was having strange behaviour outbursts, when he would wander around chanting, rather like being in a trance. He was also having classic *grand mal* epileptic attacks. He was clearly aware of the difference between the two types of attack.

Having arrived in Britain, he was started on anti-epileptic drugs for the *grand mal* epilepsy. This resulted in some decrease of the attacks. It was shortly after this that he came into contact with Christians, through whose influence he gave his life to the Lord.

Now, whenever he was in a meeting where the Holy Spirit began to move powerfully, he would manifest one or other of these two distinct forms of attack. He was prayed for on a number of occasions with a real diminution in the frequency of the attacks, but no cure. Even praying in his home, and destroying the pictures of his former heathen deities, though it caused much rumpus and manifestation of demonic presence, did not lead to his being set totally free.

Away at a church holiday, he again began with the strange trance-like forms of attack during a time of praise with some other young single people. Every time the praise began he would go off in his trance-like state. It was most disruptive. A couple of older Christians were called in, including the Asian pastor from his church, who received a clear word from the Lord that these attacks still had their hold on Ali because he was keeping part of his life to himself, and resisting the Lordship of Christ in these areas. Faced with this, Ali let go and the strange trances stopped.

He is still on the anti-epileptic drugs for the classic *grand mal* attacks. We are asking the Lord now whether or not these have also been dealt with. If they have been, then he can follow safely the normal medical approach for coming off these drugs, i.e. if he has one year without attacks, then he can cut the pills down slowly, and then come off them altogether.

Delusions; Voices and Behaviour Disorders

Sam was brought along to the fellowship by some concerned people. He had turned up on their doorstep, looking in awful shape, saying that he had just come out of a mental hospital. He apparently had nowhere to go. It was quite difficult trying to piece the true story together. We were not sure what drugs, if any, he was on. It seemed from what he was saying that he probably had been having treatment recently for a schizophrenic episode. He would hardly communicate at all.

His new found friends began to pray. They quickly came across some clear demonic problems as they prayed with Sam, and then asked me if I would pray for him. I did so briefly, but was immediately aware that this fellow was going to need a lot of tender loving care if he was to become a whole person again. He had all the marks of those who have been institutionalised by being in mental hospital for a prolonged spell. I encouraged the pair who had taken him in to give him loving care, but only in small doses. They were not to spend all of their free time with him. I knew that this sort of person would soak up all the attention that anyone would give him, and more!

On a couple of subsequent occasions we prayed in meetings. Mainly the praying was done by those who had taken him in, within their own home. Things began to change. Sam's dress and personal hygiene began remarkably to improve. He began to speak much more clearly. He gave his life to the Lord, and shortly after was baptised. He continued to improve. Then he was baptised in the Holy Spirit. This slow miracle had so far taken about three months to blossom.

During most of this time I hardly saw Sam, except at a distance in meetings. I knew that the others would call for help if they felt that they needed any. About four months after I had first met him, I found myself on the opposite side of a table tennis table from him at the church holiday. Five minutes later, totally wiped off the table by his vastly superior skill, I found myself thinking, 'This young man is completely transformed'.

Those thoughts were not just the battered remains of a wounded pride, defeated at table tennis! I realised that every impression I had originally formed in my mind about this young man had to be totally revised. He was now clearly becoming the man that Jesus had all along intended him to be. His physical vigour, his mental alertness, but above all his spiritual perception, had all been transformed by the renewal of his mind.

It would be good to take a little time to look at some of the more major psychiatric disturbances that quite frequently come the way of those who are counselling. It is useful to have some guidelines to help one understand what the medical personnel feel is going on. This may also provide insight as to why they are treating a person in the manner, or with the drugs, that they are.

We must realise that each of the things that I mention briefly here would take a full chapter in any standard textbook of psychiatry. This is no more than a very rudimentary attempt to help us know how other professions view a person's 'illness'. It is also a clear warning to those counsellors who find themselves in areas where they have no competence to deal with the problem. If that is the case, call a halt to your counselling. Then get in some help. Never be afraid to admit that you need help, possibly of a professional nature.

A situation I was involved in some time ago will help to clarify this. A young man whom Felicity and I had known well for some years came to live with us. He had always had a trust in the Lord, but was never particularly known for having an active witness. Now, however, it seemed that he did nothing but speak to everyone about Christ. He was out on the streets in his spare time, passing out tracts, and stopping people to tell them about Christ. He was often warning us all of Christ's imminent coming. For a couple of days this zeal seemed very good to us. But his behaviour became more and more bizarre. Sometimes the things that he said did not make sense. Sometimes he seemed almost 'possessed' by his message. He also began doing strange things around the house that did not tally with someone who was genuinely on fire for the Lord.

Within a couple of weeks it was clear he was living with a number of delusions. His ideas became even stranger, and then he passed into a frank psychotic episode, with his behaviour being so bizarre that he needed medical help to come back down to earth! We did not have any success when we tried encouraging him to be prayed with over his behaviour. He seemed to have no insight at all into the fact that the way he was behaving was abnormal.

There is much that we still do not know. We do better to admit our lack of knowledge than to plough on and end up damaging the person that we are trying to help. This will also inevitably damage our own credibility.

Nearly all who have been involved in counselling for some time will have come across situations such as I have described above. Even while we may have a pretty shrewd idea that the root of the problem is primarily spiritual, we should be happy to see the person get the medical help that they need when confronted with our own inability to help them. We may then later, away from the pressure of the acute episode, be able to get to the root of the problem. Alternatively, the Holy Spirit may deal with it during prayer, without us ever really knowing what was going on.

It is similar when we come to people who are hearing voices. From a psychiatric viewpoint there is quite a bit that can be learned from how these voices speak to the person. Do they try to frighten him? Do they come from standard sources of communication such as the radio or television? Do they claim to watch the person?

While these questions may help to clarify the psychiatric diagnosis, they usually do little to define what is the source of the problem. It is here that we need to know from the Lord what is going on with the person.

Earlier on I described the young girl who suffered from abdominal pain and blackouts. We only knew how to help her because the Lord showed my wife exactly what to ask. We need the gifts of the Holy Spirit in our work.

Far too much Christian counselling is just a slightly spiritualised version of what is easily available elsewhere. We should not be trying to do in an amateur fashion what other highly competent professionals have spent years in learning to do. Our authority comes solely from what we have learned in the Lord. This does not deny the validity of other approaches and techniques. Rather, it is a statement that we should not pretend to be expert in areas in which we have had no real training. We can, however, give much in those areas in which we have actually learnt much from experience.

It may have already become apparent from some of the stories that I have told that there is a basic distinction between those people who recognise that they have a problem, and those who don't. The young man in the example above clearly did not recognise himself as acting in any way strangely. This condition would medically be viewed as *psychotic*.

Where people do have some insight into what is wrong with them, often actually coming for help to deal with this, the condition is termed *neurotic*. Unfortunately, the term neurotic has come to mean something entirely different in ordinary usage by non-medical people. Medically, to term someone as neurotic in no way implies either that they are a nuisance (though they may be!), or that they could 'snap out of it' if they so wished. It just means that the person has a condition which is more amenable to help and therapy (whether psychotherapy or counselling help, or from drug therapy), and into which they have some insight.

It has been a major advance in the treatment of psychotic conditions (i.e. those in which the patient has little or no insight), to have certain drugs known as psychotropic or mind active drugs, which have helped to bring people under more reasonable control. Unfortunately, these drugs rarely, if ever, seem to effect a cure. Rather, they limit the more bizarre manifestations of people's behaviour, and as such render the people more acceptable to society at large. It also means that many people suffering from psychotic illnesses need not be detained in mental hospitals, but can be safely and adequately treated while staying at home in an environment which is much more normal for them.

There are problems, however, with these drugs. As with all medications they do have side effects. Sometimes these side effects are themselves quite nasty. They also seem to reduce the person's ability to communicate very effectively. (This, one must remember, may have already been severely reduced by the illness.) Many people on large doses of these drugs seem to be reduced to mere zombies, often talking only about themselves and their illness.While this is undoubtedly better for them than being in the frankly 'crazy' phase of the illness, it is no cure! We need cures. Whether or not medicine finds a cure, or pyschotherapy finds a psychological root that it can expose, we know that Jesus can heal! We need to reach out for the healing power of God to see these people's lives transformed. God is not just in the business of making neurotics whole. He is also wonderfully restoring those who are psychotic.

I would suggest that a useful guideline in trying to decide whether or not one can begin to help a person is to see if they have a neurotic illness or a psychotic type. If it is neurotic, then do try to step in. Selwyn Hughes, in his excellent book on counselling, *A Friend in Need*, tells of some fascinating research that has shown that tender loving care by a concerned friend can be more effective than professional psychotherapy in dealing with this type of condition.

If, however, the condition of the person is psychotic, i.e. they have no insight into their situation, or if you feel that there are irrational or other rather bizarre aspects of a person's story that make you anxious, then do refer them to someone more experienced and with medical knowledge. A Christian doctor or psychiatrist can often help immensely in sorting out whether a problem has a spiritual, physical, or emotional basis. They may or may not have the faith to reach out to God to see the condition dealt with. Just because you call in professional help, do not stop praying. And do not stop responding to what the Holy Spirit tells you to do.

Practical Cautions

This is probably the place to add a word or two of caution for those who are likely to be involved with this sort of ministry. Firstly, we do need to be aware of the help the person may be receiving from medical personnel. This will tend to make us aware of what is happening in response to prayer and what is happening because of the medication that they are on.

Anti-epileptic drugs can themselves cause epilepsy if they are withdrawn too suddenly. They should always be cut down slowly. It is far better for patients to do this with the knowledge of their doctor. We should not be in the business of antagonising those in the medical profession. But neither do we need to be intimidated by them. Most will not believe in the realm of the spirit, much less the supernatural as evidenced by miracles. So we have a loving responsibility to convince them through the genuineness of what they see. Recognise, though, that seeing is not believing. Do not be disappointed when medical people often choose not to believe even when powerful miracles have occurred under their noses.

Jesus said that it would be like this. 'If they do not listen to Moses and the prophets, neither will they be persuaded if someone rises from the dead' (Lk. 16:31).

A second area of caution is that of being over-involved in ministering deliverance. I think that it was CS Lewis who said that the devil would like to get us to fall into one of two opposite errors. Either we can begin to see demons behind every problem and difficulty that arises, or we can in practice believe that they do not exist, and do not influence our lives and surrounding circumstances at all. Both viewpoints are wrong.

Demons are very real, but they are not the cause of every problem. Most of our problems we bring on ourselves. Demons attack where we provide opportunity through sin (Eph. 4:27). Where a problem or illness does have a clear demonic component, then we need to know how to deal with it. We have the authority that Jesus gave to us. We shold be familiar with Scriptures such as:

'Behold, I give you authority to tread upon serpents and scorpions, and over all the power of the enemy, and nothing shall injure you' (Lk. 10:19).

'All authority has been given to Me in Heaven and on earth. Go therefore and make disciples of all the nations' (Mt. 28:18-19).

'And I will give you the keys of the kingdom of heaven; and whatever you shall bind on earth shall be bound in heaven, and whatever you shall loose on earth shall be loosed in heaven' (Mt. 16:19).

'When He had disarmed the rulers and authorities, He made a public display of them, having triumphed over them through Him' (Col. 2:15).

Jesus, in fighting Satan, used the word of God (Mt. 4). We need to be able to wield these Scriptures in such a way that Satan knows he is fighting a battle he has already lost. His main weapon against us is our ignorance of the power and authority that we have. He will lie to us about our authority: he will even try to quote Scripture to us, as he did to Jesus, to make us feel that we cannot possibly win the fight against him.

When we know that we are going to come against demonic powers we do well to minister in pairs. One person can always be praying while the other one is counselling or praying against the demonic powers. Jesus sent his disciples out in pairs to preach and to heal.

The power of ministering together is being recaptured by the Church in the present move of the Holy Spirit. Seldom now do those who come to teach or preach in our church come on their own. Usually they come with others who are also expecting to find a way to minister in the situation. I know that when I go to preach somewhere, I feel very vulnerable if I have not been able to arrange for others to come also. They are not only an active back-up in prayer, but also a tremendous help in ministry. Particularly, I find that others may exercise various of the gifts of the Holy Spirit in such a way that it will break open the meeting for people to receive what the Lord has given me to teach or to preach.

Another area of caution to watch for in all counselling, and especially when dealing with demonic powers, is that of emotions and emotionalism taking over from genuine Holy Spirit ministry. The realm of the spirit and the realm of the emotions are very close to each other. This is particularly true of some of the visible manifestations that the Holy Spirit uses to bring deep healing to people.

Many are now familiar with watching a person fall over (usually called 'resting in the Spirit' or 'being slain in the Spirit'), when somebody prays for them. Such manifestations are well recorded in all times of revival. Reading descriptions of the early Quaker and Methodist meetings makes one realise that these things are not in any sense new. What possibly is new is the scale and frequency with which we now see such things. Also many who minister powerfully in the Holy Spirit expect such things to happen when they pray for people, and this expectation brings a greater release of these manifestations of the Holy Spirit.

Tears may be a sign of deep happiness, of deep remorse, or even of the Holy Spirit moving in a person in a powerful way without either of the above two emotions being felt. I can remember two distinct occasions, separated by approximately twelve years, when people have laid hands on me in a meeting, and I have found myself crying uncontrollably for long periods of time. I still do not know exactly what the Holy Spirit was doing inside me on either occasion. What I do know is that I have seen a greater release of the power of the Holy Spirit through me following both of these incidents.

Once on praying with a young man to be baptised in the Holy Spirit he began to laugh so much and so loudly (as did I!) that we had to be escorted out of the meeting because we were disrupting others. Yet other times, laughter may only touch our emotions, and actually end up hindering us from receiving what the Lord wants to say to us.

Our emotions can again play havoc with us in counselling between members of the opposite sex. Sometimes I have seen a woman praying for a man and stroking his hair while praying for him. Speaking for myself, I would find that far from helpful in encouraging me to keep my mind on the Lord! There may easily be a place for touch and warmth being expressed in the counselling situation, but it is much safer man to man or woman to woman. In medicine it is generally viewed as unwise for a male doctor to examine a female patient without a chaperone present. Similarly, when the Holy Spirit begins to strip off some of the emotional veneer that people have covered themselves with, we need to be sensitive, while being sensible, not to become emotionally entangled. This does not mean that we cannot empathise with a person, but we are trying to be wise in guarding our hearts. Too many godly men have begun by trying to help a vulnerable young woman in need, and ended up sexually entangled with her.

There is one final area that I think should be mentioned while we are looking at these cautions. As we open up our lives to seek to bless others, we will find that more and more people come to us for help. There sometimes does not seem to be any end to those who are needing counsel. On top of this they begin arriving at our homes and offices at increasingly inconvenient times, often desperate for help. It is tempting to feel that we cannot just leave them, but perhaps neither can we really spare the time at that moment to help them.

Felicity and I used to find this often happening to us.

A rare evening with nothing planned would suddenly be interrupted by someone arriving at the door whose problem was so urgent that it could only be dealt with right now by us! (How easily our pride fools us into thinking that we are indispensable!) Maybe we had been involved in a couple of meetings that had ended rather late. Tonight was going to be an early night. You sense that this may take rather a long time!

It may actually be appropriate to ask them to come back the following evening! If it has kept this long, another day is not likely to cause much harm. We need to be aware that one of Satan's devices is to 'wear down the saints of the Highest One' (Dan. 7:25). Tiredness itself begins to be a hindrance, not only to ministry, but also to getting up to meet with the Lord the next day. If we are not sensible about when we go to bed, then we will not be able to be sensible about when we get up. Benjamin Franklin's old adage still makes a lot of sense:

Early to bed, Early to rise
Makes a man healthy, wealthy and wise.

These comments on practical pitfalls that we want to avoid obviously apply right across the board, and not just to dealing with epilepsy and psychotic illness. It is as we find ourselves beginning to help folk with more serious problems, that we need to exercise even greater care in their counsel. It is one thing to help a person through a minor upset; it is another thing to find yourself involved where other experts have possibly already tried and failed. If we are not to bring Christian counselling into disrepute, then we must be sensible in how we deal with people. At the end of the day, we are going to know the effective Christian counsellors by their fruit.

Those involved in Christian ministry should be honest enough, and critical enough, to ask themselves how things are going. We do no one we are seeking to help any good by just hoping that they are getting better. If we are genuinely moving in the power of the Holy Spirit, then people should be clearly coming back to full mental, emotional, physical, and spiritual health. If this is not happening then we need to find out why. We also need to find out quickly, before we begin damaging people.

A friend of mine who works as a consultant psychotherapist tells me that most of his work is with people who have already been ministered to by others! He ends up with other peoples' failures. Often these people, who have deep psychological and spiritual needs, have only had a quick prayer at the end of a healing meeting. They have been helped temporarily, but the problems recur. What has gone wrong?

One might pray for a person with moderately severe arthritis in the knees. There is a marked improvement following prayer. But when you see the person at another meeting six months later, the arthritis is as bad as ever. Why?

That person needed not just prayer, but advice on losing weight. If we see people healed, but leave them in the same situation that caused the mess in the first place, then we should hardly be surprised if the problem recurs. It is precisely because we are so often unwilling to get involved in the ongoing pastoral needs of people, that we see them coming again and again for ministry.

12: The Power of Signs and Wonders

'For I will not presume to speak of anything except what Christ has accomplished through me, resulting in the obedience of the Gentiles by word and deed, in the power of signs and wonders, in the power of the Holy Spirit' (Rom. 15:18-19).

Many periods of Bible history are filled with accounts of the supernatural power of God. However there is no portion of the Bible like the Gospels for the sheer variety and power of the manifestations of God. God's vessel in this great outpouring of the Holy Spirit was of course His Son, the Lord Jesus Christ.

Jesus knew the power of signs and wonders. He seemed quite unashamed in his use of the power of the miraculous to open people to the message that He was bringing. He knew that a miracle would never make a person a believer, but He also knew that it would make many people stop and listen.

'If I do not do the works of My Father, do not believe Me; but if I do them, though you do not believe Me, believe the works, that you may know and understand that the Father is in Me, and I in the Father' (Jn. 10:37-38). If ever there was a great preacher it was Jesus. But even He did not rely just on the power of his preaching. He knew that the miracles would draw people to come and learn from God.

Miracles are signposts to help to show people the way. Of themselves they do not prove anything. It is certainly true that there can be false miracles, but this is no reason for not desiring the real thing. Anything worthwhile is going to be counterfeited by the enemy. In John 20:30, the apostle tells us that he describes the 'signs' that Jesus did, 'so that you may believe that Jesus is the Christ, the Son of God; and that believing you may have life in His name.' Signs do not of themselves make us believers, but they can certainly help.

If Jesus needed to use them, then it is pretty likely that we will also want to. In another place in talking about casting out demons, Jesus told the crowds that 'if I cast out demons by the finger of God, then the kingdom of God has come upon you' (Lk. 11:20). Signs and wonders are a manifestation of the Kingdom that are very difficult to ignore. A signpost demands that we make a choice as to what direction we are going to take.

Jesus did not expect those who listened to him to accept what He was saying only on the basis of what they heard. Again and again He would point them to the signs, not as proof, but as confirmation. When John the Baptist wanted to know if this was really the Christ who was to come, Jesus sent back a message to him, 'the blind receive sight, the lame walk, the lepers are cleansed, and the deaf hear, the dead are raised up, the poor have the gospel preached to them. And blessed is he who keeps from stumbling over Me' (Lk. 7:22-23).

Jesus would often refer to the miracles that He did as 'the works' that the Father had given Him to do (Jn. 5:36, 7:3, 9:3-4, 10:32, 14:10-12). He viewed His own healing ministry as a natural extension of the message that He was bringing. For Jesus it would have been unthinkable that He would just preach. He wanted always to be doing the things that He saw His heavenly Father doing. And Jesus has not changed. 'Jesus Christ is the same yesterday, today, yes and forever' (Heb. 13:8).

For some years now I have been convinced that we would not see people turning to Christ on a large scale in this country without the release of God's miraculous power. In the church that I used to belong to in East London, we decided, in response to a prophetic word to us, that we would set aside a period of forty Fridays to pray and fast. During this time we began to pray in faith to God to do a new thing among us.

Near the end of that period we had a time of extensive outreach. The Lord had made it possible for us to have Ian Andrews, an evangelist with a clear healing ministry, to work with us for the first week. Many came to those meetings, and a number were clearly healed. We continued holding meetings with an emphasis on healing and found to our delight and some surprise that the Lord continued to heal. This initiated a period of rapid growth as a church. Some months later we decided that we should look back statistically at the growth of the three months during and after the mission. We found that of the 60 who had apparently come to the Lord during that time, we were still in active contact with 57, who were coming along regularly to the meetings.

This extraordinarily high percentage of people 'sticking' was in marked contrast with other periods of mission where our experience had been that six months later more than seventy-five per cent had been lost to active church involvement. There may have been a number of reasons for this apparent success. However, to us the main distinguishing feature of this time was that we were operating in the power of signs and wonders. Those converted to Christ during times of visible manifestation of God's power appear to be touched at a deeper level than those that we had previously seen coming to the Lord.

Many times within the surgery context I have seen how a demonstration of the power of God will break open patients' lives in such a way that they will want to follow Jesus. A young woman, of whom I had seen quite a bit because she had just had a baby, came in to see me one morning because she was gripped by a fear that she had acquired AIDS. She had had a blood transfusion during the summer, and now with all the publicity surrounding AIDS, and the idea that some people catch it through transfusions rather than through homosexual practices, she was terrified that she had it. There was no good medical reason for this fear. But she would not be convinced. I tried to reassure her, and arranged for her to have the appropriate tests to confirm that she did not have the disease.

Half an hour later she was back in the surgery, very distressed, demanding to see me immediately. As we talked together I was really worried that she was going over the top, and had real psychiatric problems. I offered to pray with her and told her how Jesus could set her free from the irrational fears that had gripped her. We prayed and she left the surgery.

To my delight, she turned up at church on Sunday, having accepted my invitation. During the meeting she went out for prayer with my wife and a friend. She gave her life to the Lord and was filled with the Holy Spirit.

The next morning she was at the surgery to see me. 'All of the fear has gone. Do I still need to go and have the blood tests done?'

The power of the gospel had freed her to respond to the claims of the gospel. For far too long now we have been rather ashamed of the glorious gospel that we have been given. Knowing that we could not produce the goods in the way that they did in the New Testament, we have rather tended to keep silent.

Now we can stay silent no longer. We are seeing and hearing stories from all over the world of God's healing power. The Holy Spirit is challenging us all to be a part of this unfolding drama. We too can see the power of God in our churches. What the Lord is doing in Korea, or South Africa, or Latin America, He can equally do here.

Felicity and I have often reflected on what we learnt from Dr Paul Yongghi Cho's church while we were out in Korea. Two things have subsequently become plain. One is that we often ignore the plain teaching of Scripture, and try to counsel people by human wisdom and learning. The other is that in practice we deny the power of prayer by just not praying.

So much of our counselling, or sharing the Lord with people, is in effect just a sharing of ourselves. This is fine, where our lives really tally with the word of God and the Spirit of God, but it is grossly inadequate in areas where we are ourselves deficient. By teaching people that they can themselves claim the power of God, we are in fact being of much greater help to them. As each person takes responsibility for their own condition, so they will find the desire and strength to ask the Lord for His transforming power.

As Christians, we live in a supernatural realm. We are seated with Christ in the heavenly places, far above all rule and authority and dominion and power. This is not the place for us timidly to wonder if God just might be willing to intervene in our lives or the lives of others whom He sends our way. This is the place where we, like the disciples, 'preach everywhere, while the Lord worked with them, and confirmed the word by the signs that followed' (Mk. 16-20).

It is fascinating to look at the Scriptures with this

realisation of the dependence of both the Lord Jesus and the disciples on the direct supernatural intervention of God in their daily lives. Jesus saw the release of the supernatural as an integral part of the work that His Father had given to Him to do. He sent out both his disciples, and subsequently ourselves with the same commission, 'As the Father has sent me, I also send you' (Jn. 20-21).

I think that this is the most exciting time that we could have been alive in which to serve the Lord. What a privilege it is for us both to see and participate in the things that the Lord is doing by His Spirit all over the world! With faith, we are going to see in the United Kingdom the same revival fires that God is at present pouring out in so many other parts of the world.

13 The Needy you have Always

Wednesdays used to be a half day for me. As I only had an evening surgery on that day, I would normally reserve the time to catch up on things that needed doing within the church or in Caring Professions Concern.

I knew this Wednesday would be a bit different because I was having to cover the whole day. Morning surgery was quiet, and I had only one visit to do after the surgery. This was a woman who had apparently been drinking too much.

When I got to her home I quickly found that there was more to the situation than at first met the eye. This mother of three was absolutely desperate. One of her children was also at home and confirmed much of the following story. Her husband had gone off with another woman, and was now trying to get the children to treat this new woman as 'mother'. Whenever he did come home he would sexually abuse the real mother, and constantly make callously crude remarks to her. On one occasion recently he had even tried to molest a friend of hers who had been in the house. To make it worse, the new woman was actually preferred by at least one of the children. Her world was falling in on top of her and her response was to turn to drink.

I tried then, and on several subsequent occasions to help her. I talked about the Lord Jesus with her. I offered to pray. I encouraged her to forgive. But I could not find any way to get through to her that there was hope – that God could step into a situation like this.

It was halfway into the afternoon of the same day. I had gone to the church office to get some other work done. The phone rang, and it was the practice to say that another woman patient of ours was shouting and screaming outside her home. The neighbours had taken the children in and had called us.

I dashed over as quickly as I could. I had no idea what to expect. On arrival I found this young woman sitting in her living room, sobbing her eyes out. The neighbour still had the children.

'He promised me,' she cried, 'He promised me that today he would watch the kids for me while I went to an important appointment, and then he left me stranded. He's always doing that to me.'

At this point the husband came in, and confirmed that the substance of what his wife had said was true. In seconds they were shouting at each other. As I calmed them down to dialogue, it turned out that constant 'betrayal' of promises by the husband had led her to a state where she couldn't – and didn't want to – cope. She had had enough. She wanted him to be stranded with the children for a while to see what it was like.

Again I tried to tell them how true love and forgiveness in Christ could provide a foundation for putting the family back together. But neither party wanted to be the one to change. The household was now calm, but I knew that nothing permanent had yet been solved. I urged them to join me at church, or to come and see me in the surgery again to chat further, but sadly they did neither.

Arriving home at the end of the evening surgery, I was about to have a bite to eat before going out to a meeting when the phone rang again. This time it was the practice telephone answering service to say that a teenage girl was shouting and out of control in her home and her parents did not know what do do. Slightly fed up with the possibility of seeing another raving person on the same day, I bundled myself into the car, hoping to deal with this one quickly.

It was not to be. The seventeen-year-old daughter was shouting the place down, and my appearing was just an excuse for more shouting. The whole family was in pandemonium, with everybody shouting at everyone else. The mother told me that she was thinking of committing suicide. Another daughter told me that her mum was always saying such things. No wonder the seventeen-year-old was shouting her head off.

I asked all of the other family members to leave the room, and sat down with the teenager. Slowly she stopped shouting, and then we were able actually to have a sensible conversation. Just a little earlier that evening her mother had again told her she was going to commit suicide. The daughter had enough problems of her own, and hearing this, decided that the only way she could herself call out for help was to begin shouting. Something inside seemed to flip and she could not stop or control herself.

I now brought the family together. We tried to talk together sensibly. The father sat to one side with the sort of look on his face that said, 'I've already given up on this lot.' Our talking really got us nowhere. Obviously I asked them to come back to see me. But they never did.

As I look back on that day, my heart still longs to see everyone helped. We read of Jesus that all who came to Him He healed. But they did have to come to Him. There must have been so many who would not come. I am reminded of His words to the people of Jerusalem, 'How often I wanted to gather your children together, the way a hen gathers her chicks under her wings, and you were unwilling' (Mt. 23:37).

Then, as now, for people to receive help, they have to want it. The call of the gospel is still 'whosoever will may come'. Our responsibility is to let them know of the glorious possibility of freedom. We must continue to tell those who come our way that Jesus can meet them at the point of their deepest need.

An Introduction to Caring Professions Concern

Caring Professions Concern, of which Dr Tony Dale is the General Secretary, is an organisation formed to help encourage and build up Christians who are serving the Lord in the health care and allied professions.

A twofold mandate has been given to CPC: the prophetic and the pastoral. Our desire is to reach all those in the caring professions and through them to bring wholeness in Christ to the people of this country.

The Prophetic Concern

'Without a vision the people perish' and without a vision the caring professions will also perish. The signs of this process are everywhere. The prophetic voice needs to be heard speaking with clarity to caring professionals who are prepared to live up to their high calling in Christ.

Radical questions need to be asked, such as: Why is there so much emphasis on pathology and not on prevention? Who cares about the whole person? Is the new emphasis in health care on holistic medicine to be bypassed by the Christian caring community? Should not the church be taking the initiative in bringing authentic wholeness i.e. salvation, to the people of our generation? How can mere social action deal with society's or the individual's ills without also actively aiming to change people's hearts?

The essential burden of CPC - concern for the whole person - recognises the intrinsic worth of all individuals before God their Creator. This immediately brings confrontation with the humanistic trends prevalent in the caring professions. Why isn't the Christain conscience more vocal at the 'slaughter of the innocents' in abortion? Where is the line to be drawn with the handicapped? At what level of defect or retardation will we next decide - with godlike presumption - that 'this one hasn't the right to live'? How do we bring wholeness and healing into the counselling situation? If we truly care for our patients and clients, should we not naturally tell them how Christ can make them whole?

Do Christians care that significant inroads are being made into all the caring professions, not only by humanism, but also by spiritualism and eastern ideologies such as transcendental meditation? We need present-day 'Elijahs' to declare forthrightly to this generation that the humanistic ethic is creating, in effect, a modern Baal at whose shrine the caring professions are dutifully 'worshipping', causing offence to the Living God.

Exploration of the Biblical understanding of illness, whether physical, emotional, mental or spiritual is leading to a much greater expectation of the supernatural power of God being released within the professional context. We can take a clear stand for Christ.

The Pastoral Concern

Working within the caring professions inevitably produces its own pressure on our lives. Because of this, CPC seeks to provide an opportunity to bring healing from Christ to the 'healers'. Within a context of mutual trust and sensitivity, Christian professionals can discuss not only difficult problems cropping up within their own lives, but difficulties in their work.

Christian professionals, working within the context of their local church, can provide a valuable focus for exploring the practice of whole person medicine. In some areas this has meant establishing Primary Care Centres attached to local church fellowships. Then regions have pioneered Christian counselling services to serve local GPs, social services, churches, etc. Neighbourhood care schemes, actively involving Christians from local churches, have extended the Christian professionals' ability to bring wholeness to those in the community. In this way committed members of a local church fellowship are able to act as a catalyst in the development of care within the context of the local Christian community.

Drawing in professional and lay people within a church context is an exciting extension of the biblical context of being sent out to 'preach the gospel and heal the sick'. Under the authority and stimulus of the local church, a belief in the present-day power of God is leading many to see the miraculous beginning to happen.

The encouragement of learning from other Christian professionals helps make personal witness of the Lord Jesus an integral part of our daily work. The release of the gifts of the Holy Spirit within us provides the power for this witness to be effective.

The Way Forward

For the above concepts to become reality, more people need to become actively involved. Such participation requires a two-fold focus: prayer and finance. To support full-time office staff, to run regional conferences with the support of the local Christian community, and to bring about a Christian perspective for the health care and social services, demands a deep level of commitment.

Our goal, in working together, is to win the caring professions for Jesus. Social workers, doctors, nurses, care attendants, are among the many caring professionals who are learning that by standing together they can be more effective for Christ. Although our focus is the caring professions, all those who share our vision and goal are welcome - both as members and at any of our conferences. In this way, we can see 'the kingdom of this world become the kingdom of our Lord and His Christ' (Rev. 11:15).

If you would like to be involved in this exciting vision please write to:

Dr Tony Dale, MB BS
Caring Professions Concern
The King's Centre
High Street
Aldershop
Hants GU11 1DJ   Tel No. 0252-317277.

FORGIVE AND RESTORE

Don Baker

When a member of God's family, in this case a loved pastor, goes seriously off the rails in his personal life, the questions looms large, What should the church do about it? Is it a matter for the church leadership only? Should the wayward member be asked to leave or just relieved of responsibility? What should the congregation be told?

This book is a remarkable account of how one church dealt with such a highly charged and emotional crisis. It records in honest detail the ebb and flow of hope and despair, uncertainty and humanity, and relying throughout on biblical principles, it picks its way through a tangled mess to find a place of healing and restoration again.

WHEN YOU PRAY

Reginald East

Spiritual renewal has awakened in many Christians a deeper longing to know God more intimately. Prayer is the place where we personally meet God, yet it is often treated simply as the means for making requests for our needs, and offering our stilted, dutiful thanks. In this practical guide to prayer, Reginald East shows how we can establish a prayer relationship with God which is both spiritually and emotionally satisfying. Through understanding God and ourselves better, prayer can truly become an encounter with God, where we relax into Him, enjoy Him, listen as well as talk to Him and adventure into discovering His heart of love.

If you wish to receive *regular information* about *new books*, please send your name and address to:

London Bible Warehouse
PO Box 123
Basingstoke
Hants RG23 7NL

Name..

Address ....

....

....

....

I am especially interested in:
☐ Biographies
☐ Fiction
☐ Christian living
☐ Issue related books
☐ Academic books
☐ Bible study aids
☐ Children's books
☐ Music
☐ Other subjects